REDISCOVERING THE PRAIRIES

JOURNEYS BY DOG, HORSE & CANOE

BY NORMAN HENDERSON

——

DRAWINGS BY ROBERT COOK

Victoria · Calgary · Vancouver

TouchWood Editions 2005
1 2 3 4 5 / 08 07 06 05

TouchWood Editions
#108 – 17665 66A Avenue
Surrey, BC V3S 2A7
www.touchwoodeditions.com

Library and Archives Canada Cataloguing in Publication
Henderson, Norman, 1960-
      Rediscovering the Prairies : journeys by dog, horse & canoe / by Norman Henderson ; drawings by Robert Cook.
Previously ed. published under title: Rediscovering the Great Plains.
Includes bibliographical references and index.
ISBN 1-894898-36-2
      1. Transportation--Qu'Appelle River Valley (Sask. and Man.).
2. Transportation--Great Plains. 3. Qu'Appelle River Valley (Sask. and Man.)--Description and travel. 4. Great Plains--Description and travel.
5.Henderson, Norman, 1960- --Travel--Qu'Appelle River Valley (Sask. and Man.). I. Henderson, Norman, 1960- . Rediscovering the Great Plains.
II. Title.
FC3517.4.H46 2005   917.124'4   C2005-904964-2

Printed in Canada on 100% post-consumer recycled paper.

TouchWood Editions acknowledges the financial support for its publishing program from the Government of Canada through the Book Publishing Industry Development Program (BPIDP), Canada Council for the Arts, and the British Columbia Arts Council.

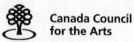

For all who love the prairies

———

As for man, his days are like grass;

he flourishes like a flower of the field;

for the wind passes over it, and it is gone,

and its place knows it no more.

—PSALM 103

Contents

Preface

THIS IS a book about dogs, horses, canoes, and, above all, about the Great Plains both old and new. It is a kind of biography, though of a landscape, rather than a person. This landscape, the Plains, is sadly misnamed, for it is rarely completely flat, and never dull. The word *prairie* has more romance and I sometimes prefer it, for I know of no landscape with more personality than North America's heartland of grass. In fact *grassland* is perhaps the most apt name of all, for it makes clear we are speaking of a living landscape. It is also an enigmatic one. Consider the seemingly fragile prairie grasses, which may rise only a few inches above the ground and flex and bend with a whisper of wind. Below the surface the roots may sink many feet deep, strong and tenacious to withstand flood, fire, or drought. The grasses are more invisible than visible, and far tougher than they seem. Immigrants to the Plains, like the native grasses, needed a mix of caution, adaptability, and deep resources to survive. This is asking for a lot, and the Great Plains of the United States and Canada were more likely than any other region to break the spirit of the newcomer.

To write a "normal" biography you read, think, and speak to others about your subject and, if you possibly can, you interview him or her in person. These techniques help to build a picture of the individual's essential spirit. I have used the identical techniques to try to understand the essence of the prairies. Well, how do you "interview" a landscape, you may fairly ask? The best way I know of is to travel through it—slowly, and as exposed to the elements as reasonably possible. In so doing, if you have eyes to see and ears to hear, and if you take time to breathe, smell, and feel the earth and sky, you begin to divine the land and its changing moods. It is not so hard if you have a little fitness, time, and patience.

This book tells the story of how, after careful preparation for each, I made three slow prairie journeys, each time re-creating an early and largely forgotten way of prairie travel. Many centuries before the Europeans arrived in the Americas, Plains peoples were travelling the grasslands on foot with only the dog to help them carry their belongings. These sturdy animals pulled a wooden drag, called a "travois," loaded with the freight of the day. The dogs and their travois are gone from firsthand memory, but with the aid of written records, I was able to resurrect both travois and travois travel. My travelling companion, Serge, the wonderdog, then helped translate the landscape to me through the wisdom of canine eyes, ears, and nose.

My second prairie journey was by canoe in the spirit of the voyageurs, the fur traders of old. In truth, the Plains are not natural canoe country, but I found the river view of the prairie landscape as rich as it was unfamiliar. Driving over straight-line Plains highways, people forget the wonders of our ever-turning prairie rivers. This, I learned, is a great misfortune.

My final journey was by horse and horse travois. Like the canoe, the horse is a Plains import but, unlike the canoe, it is marvelously well adapted to the grasslands. My horse, gentle round-bellied Tiny, guided me to an equine understanding of the prairies. On her back, seated high above the Plains, I was a king among men.

Of course the Plains are a vast landscape, and if your intention is to travel slowly you must restrict your route accordingly. I confined my journeys to along, within, and near to the Qu'Appelle Valley in the Canadian Plains, but much of what I learned and experienced there is equally valid from Texas to Alberta, wherever some natural elements of the Great Plains remain. In fact, I would go further and say that the lessons of the Plains are most often also the lessons of the South American Pampas and the Eurasian Steppes. So, to enrich the narrative, I have sometimes made reference to the observations of those familiar with these two great temperate grassland sisters to the Plains, for most Plains people know little of the Plains' landscape kin.

The book contains two maps and eleven illustrations. Brief chapter notes give guidance for further reading. I have avoided using footnotes, but the scholar can still accurately trace any quotation or concept attributed to a named source by looking up that name in the "References" section. I have also included a section entitled "Biographic Notes," which briefly identifies the various grassland commentators or characters appearing in the text, some of whom would otherwise be unfamiliar to the reader.

Different individuals have, on occasion, asked me variants of the same basic question: what is the "real," that is, what is the deep underlying psychological motivation for anyone to go to so much time and trouble to walk, paddle, or ride the Plains? The closest thing to an answer that I know to give is that, like the mountains, the Plains are there. But, to me, the question itself is inexplicable. How could you not want to think, search, and voyage the landscape?

We know the Plains but poorly still. I invite you to journey with me, slowly, by dog, canoe, and horse, in the hope that you may know and love them a little better.

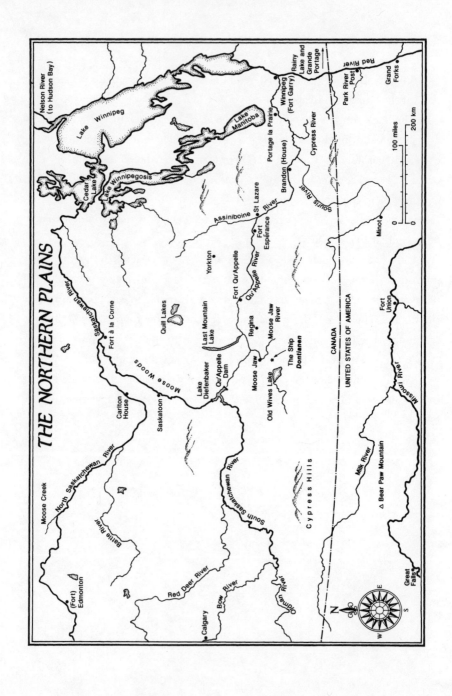

THE NORTHERN PLAINS

Nelson River (to Hudson Bay)

Lake Winnipeg

Cedar Lake

Lake Winnipegosis

Lake Manitoba

Winnipeg (Fort Garry)

Rainy Lake and Grande Portage

Red River

Park River Post

Grand Forks

Portage la Prairie

Cypress River

Brandon (House)

Souris River

St Lazare

Assiniboine River

Fort Espérance

Fort Qu'Appelle

Qu'Appelle River

Yorkton

Fort Qu'Appelle

Minot

Quill Lakes

Last Mountain Lake

Moose Jaw River

Saskatchewan River

Fort à la Corne

Regina

Moose Woods

Lake Diefenbaker

Qu'Appelle Dam

Moose Jaw

The Ship *Dontianen*

Old Wives Lake

Fort Union

Carlton House

Saskatoon

CANADA

UNITED STATES OF AMERICA

North Saskatchewan River

South Saskatchewan River

Cypress Hills

Milk River

Missouri River

Moose Creek

Battle River

Red Deer River

Bow River

Oldman River

△ Bear Paw Mountain

(Fort) Edmonton

Calgary

Great Falls

0   100 miles
0   200 km

N
W   E
S

THE QU'APPELLE VALLEY

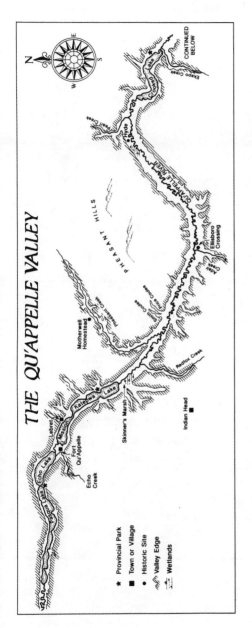

Legend:
- ★ Provincial Park
- ■ Town or Village
- ● Historic Site
- ⌒ Valley Edge
- ~ Wetlands

Pasqua Lake, Echo Lake, Echo Creek, Fort Qu'Appelle, Lebret, Mission, Katepwa Lake, Skinner's Marsh, QU'APPELLE RIVER, Motherwell Homestead, Pheasant Creek, PHEASANT HILLS, Jumping Deer Creek, Redfox Creek, Indian Head, Ash Creek, Ellisboro Crossing, Hyde, Bell Creek, Cowan Lake, Ekapo Creek, CONTINUED BELOW

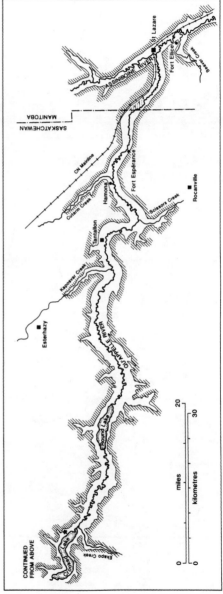

CONTINUED FROM ABOVE, Cowan Lake, Ekapo Creek, Round Lake, QU'APPELLE RIVER, Esterhazy, Kaposvar Creek, Tantallon, Cutarm Creek, Harmons, Fort Espérance, Scissors Creek, Rocanville, CN Mainline, SASKATCHEWAN / MANITOBA, Fort Ellice, ASSINIBOINE RIVER, St. Lazare, Beaver Creek

miles 0 20
kilometres 0 30

NIGHT VISION

O F   T H E   M O O N L I T   P R A I R I E S   B Y   T R A I N

IT WAS in the great shaking dome car of the Canadian transcontinental that I saw how blind many people are to the power of the Great Plains. I was above the snaking body of the train, seated in the upper deck, encased in glass, with a full view of the horizon. For roughly nineteen hundred kilometres the train had rumbled westward from Toronto, every kilometre a curvaceous homage to unbending granite and gneiss. Lake, tree, rock; lake, tree, rock; the blood, sinew, and bone of the Precambrian Shield country slid by, endlessly repetitive, a landscape mantra percolating into the soul. Finally, about one hundred kilometres east of Winnipeg, the forest opened sharply, the track steadied and stiffened, and the train stretched out like a victorious runner. For the first time we passengers felt the full power of the locomotive; the cars shook, rattled, leaned unpredictably. Unnerved, some travellers sought the greater stability of the lower deck, a few buried heads deeper in books, others increased the volume of their conversation. When a decent interval had passed, a few more passengers sought sanctuary below.

Yet I could neither read nor speak nor sleep in that immense Plains space expanding around us. Exhilaration flowed through my body in response to our acceleration into measureless grasslands. Dry prairie air filled the cabin, firing the mind.

My thoughts turned to the time before this groaning, fuming, iron horse rocked its diesel-driven way through the pairies, to when true horses of flesh and

Night train on the prairie

sinew galloped over endless grass. From the train dome I saw the Plains people of today on a distant highway, moving from A to B in their steel and plastic boxes. Every year the new vehicle models promised to distance their owners further from their environment: automate the climate control, buffer the suspension, reduce road noise, increase reliability. Did anyone out there, Indian or immigrant, remember how to walk on the Plains?

Passengers returned to the dome car in the evening for the obligatory sunset-on-the-prairies shot. Cameras clicked, camcorders whirred, bodies jostled, and eyes and minds stayed comfortably shut to the here-and-now of the prairies as the far-distant horizon rocked to the rhythm of the train. There was little world's-edge cloud to catch and refigure the day's end light, so it was not, in fact, a memorable sunset. As dusk deepened, the travellers returned below, tourist duty complete. Many would not rise to the dome again until the mountains.

Night found me alone in the dome. Dew now softened the bite of grassland air, but the sky above was a moonless black and the stars shone with a cold, impersonal edge. Still I tasted every breath of prairie air, dreaming of earlier days, of horse, of canoe, and of dog.

The prairies are not an easy landscape. It is a natural reflex to be awed by mountains; huge and overpowering, they are a beginner's landscape. Coastlines roll a rich variety of life and change before the lazy eye. Domestic landscapes of gentle hills, wood groves, and small farms enfold a timid soul in warm security. But the prairies—like the high seas or the desert—are a challenge and a reward for the strong of spirit only. You may sicken and tire here, fall prey to loneliness and melancholy, and be driven out to seek refuge in softer lands. Or you may meet the challenge, your senses may sharpen, strengthen, and thrill, as space and landscape subtlety stretch you out like a transcontinental train at full throttle. You may rejoice in the powerful exhilaration of moving over the prairies, akin to sailing the seas, an experience of freedom bordering on intoxication. Yet this great freedom is only ever a hair's breadth away from deepest loneliness. "He's got loneliness" people would say of some half-crazed early settler, a victim of excess time and space. Plains dwellers may still suffer the curse today, but few people are brave enough to admit to loneliness, for in our society it is to admit to emotional bankruptcy.

Our landscape preferences are not mere superficial expressions of aesthetic taste; they are in part manifestations of deeply encoded survival needs. Universally people prefer the sound and sight of running water to a calm water surface; subliminally we recognize the former as oxygenated, clean, and likely safe to drink. We prefer landscapes to have a mix of open and closed space, as had the savannah landscapes our species evolved in. The open areas provide us with a view and a prospect over potential food sources and enemies, while the wooded areas offer refuge, shelter, fuel, and alternative food sources. For good reason people particularly favour living at edge locations, on a coastline or river, or on a forest boundary, for example. In such places they can draw on the resources of several environments. Much of human habitat prehistory is condensed and expressed in the design of the nooks, crannies, and vistas of our public parks and private backyards.

How distant are the prairies from our landscape ideal! Their overpowering characteristic is that they have no edge and no end; they are a space devoid of reference. A man or woman placed here is a soul dropped into an ocean. Even if you can overcome the challenge of orientation, there remains the problem of survival. On the prairies every one of the basic necessities of life is difficult to secure. Water is scarce, seasonal, and often of poor quality. Food is scarce, too. Wood for shelter, fuel, and basic tools is hard to obtain. No wonder that before the Europeans few people actually lived in the heart of the Plains. Life was easier on their edges, from where the first peoples could venture out into the open spaces, searching for buffalo and other game, and then retreat to the shelter and resources of the woods, hills, or valleys that border the prairies.

Peering out of the dome darkness, I could just make out the dim edges of the flatland; in their smoothness and perfection the prairies seemed to predate God and all his fiddling details, the fjords and deltas of creation. The rich people of the prairies look to far-away cities for culture, but what was the art of learning here in my own place? And was it really my own? Did I, a white man, even belong here? The jumbled sense of identity of my fellow prairie dwellers, anchoring themselves as Ukrainians or Swedes to lands and times far away, made me wonder if we were not estranged from this land of grass. Only the intensity of the grassland experience was certain. I recalled the puzzlement of Charles Darwin* as he reflected, a few days away from landfall in England, on the entirety of his four and a half years of world travel as naturalist on HMS *Beagle*. On September 24, 1836, he confessed in his diary that of all the wondrous landscapes he had experienced, it was the Argentinean Plains that had most captivated his mind: "In

---

* The Biographic Notes identify Darwin and other grassland commentators or characters appearing subsequently in the text.

calling up images of the past, I find that the plains of Patagonia frequently cross before my eyes; yet these plains are pronounced by all wretched and useless. They can be described only by negative characters; without habitations, without water, without trees, without mountains, they support merely a few dwarf plants. Why then, and the case is not peculiar to myself, have these arid wastes taken so firm a hold on my memory?"

I had no more understanding than Darwin did of the reasons for his fixation on the arid grasslands of the south, but I shared his fascination for plains landscapes. Moreover, unlike Darwin, I had grown up under a grassland sky; I was a child of open space and geometry. Could I not therefore escape the bonds of treeism and mountainism that obscured his English vision? Surely the Plains could be understood in terms of what they were, rather than what they were not, in positives rather than in negatives. Should we describe a forest as a grassless waste, or a landscape of mountains as a barrens devoid of horizontals? For years I had lived far away from the prairies in a foreign land. In that time I had, inexplicably, become convinced that I had never really understood the grasslands, that I had never really seen them. Equally, inexorably, the need to try to understand the landscape of my birth had grown. Like Darwin, I could not forget; like Darwin, I do not know why.

Perhaps the old ways of prairies travel might provide the landscape entrée that I sought. Long before this rail journey I had been pondering the idea of choosing a prairie route and travelling it in the old ways, at a human pace, with dog, or horse, or even canoe, as a shield against loneliness and as an aid to prairie rediscovery. I could not hope to walk with the mind and through the landscape of a Dog Age Plains Indian—I am a white man marinated in Western science and thought. But I could study the old travel techniques and learn to travel in the best possible way. Had I not accomplished just that in choosing the train over the plane or car in this journey from Toronto to the West? Already the train, winding slowly through the backyards, junkyards, and industrial parks of central Canada, had taught me more about my country than any highway-bound automobile could have. I knew little of canoes, less of dogs, and nothing of horses, but this seemed all the more reason to learn.

The route would have to be carefully bounded. I could hope to understand the greater Plains whole, the vast sweep of grass from Alberta to Mexico, only by apprenticeship in the small and particular. It would be best to seek to know one limited area well. Too often we pride ourselves on the breadth of our geographic experience, on having travelled far and seen much; by ranging widely we impress our friends and ourselves, the shallowness of our worldly experience unremarked upon, even as our sense of home place atrophies. I could learn more by seeing, smelling, feeling, and listening to the same place on foot, from canoe, and from horseback than by pursuit of new lands. I needed to travel not widely but mindfully, reflectively.

I also needed somewhere old and native. This was a problem, for almost everything on the prairies is new and foreign: wheat from the Middle East, caraganas from central Asia, investment from Japan, whites from Europe. Even most dung beetles on the prairies are foreigners. Still, amid all this change, there are a few places where the natural and the old are not entirely expunged and forgotten.

It was now moonlit darkness as the train slowed and the cars rumbled and scraped up against one another, steel rubbing hard on steel. We were descending into the broad Assiniboine Valley. Slowly we descended to valley alluvium, then rolled on northward through a ghostly moon-shadowed floodplain. At the village of St. Lazare we turned west and into the Qu'Appelle Valley. Briefly the train was content on the bottomlands, but soon it angled northward and began the slow climb up the long gradient that cut the north valley wall. Dimly visible, the twisting river below reflected the moonshine above in pale flashes. My mind's eye hurried upstream, running the length of the valley. This was the place.

The Qu'Appelle Valley is a great burrowing from the end of the last ice age. Here, about fourteen thousand years ago, the continental ice sheet stalled for a few centuries during its northern retreat from the warming climate. Vast volumes of meltwater flowed west to east across the ice sheet face, cutting deep into the belly of the Plains. I stared out at the great empty valley, approximately two kilometres across and nearly ninety metres deep, and tried to imagine it over-flowing with ice water and the blue-tinged berg-bits of supercompressed glacial ice. Only the thin shimmering line of the river bore testimony to the mighty floodwaters of the past. From this distance the remnant river, only twenty-five metres across, seemed unworthy of the great valley inheritance bequeathed it by its glacial forebear.

The Qu'Appelle River's birth is now modern and unnatural, by Caesarean cut—the controlled outflow from a dam at Lake Diefenbaker five hundred kilome-tres to the west forms the modest headwaters of the river—and the past century has witnessed countless man-made intrusions into the life of the valley and its plant and animal inhabitants. But the valley remains rich in native wildlife and flora, bear and beaver, poplar and cacti. The many tributary ravines that reach far north and south of the great meltwater cut remain, often, largely undamaged. Most precious of all are the patches of native grassland on the hillslopes and on the forgotten headlands along the valley's edge, too awkwardly placed to plough. Here the old grass, the prairie wool, is still bound tight to the soil, thick and springy underfoot, impervious to drought.

On the plain above the valley an agro-grid holds sway, the angular horizontal geometry of farm and road echoing the vertical rigidity of modern urban archi-tecture. But cut into and below the vast agro-industrial machine the Qu'Appelle River still casually throws its great mile-wide meanders across the valley floor. On some modern maps the main employ of the river is as a minor political bound-ary, but I could still use it as the unifying pathway it once had been. For the valley is rich in human as well as natural history. Fur traders and explorers paddled the river, horsemen and women rode the valley trails, and Dog Age peoples lived and walked the valley for millennia.

Clouds rolled over the moon and it was deepest prairie night as I meditated over my plans to revisit the Dog Age. I would build a traditional dog travois, the wood and skin load-bearing rack dragged by generations of Plains dogs before the horse was even a Plains rumor. I would search out a Plains dog, and then, in preparation for a long journey, train it to travois on the valley slopes and in the tributary ravines that the locals here called "coulees." It would be the opening act of a biography of the prairie landscape. If all went well, canoe and horse travel would follow and deep-etch my understanding of earth, grass, and prairie waters; I would re-create all the old ways of prairie travel that predated the train. Research, training, and logistics would demand a year's preparation for each journey. As part of my apprenticeship in landscape knowledge I would read widely of the peoples who had lived and travelled in the past in the Plains' grassland realm, and also of those who knew the other great temperate grasslands, the Steppes and the Pampas. What wondrous Plains learning, what unexpected prairie adventure, might lie ahead? The dome car shook through the night prairies, heading northwest, as excitement kept me staring blindly back over the rear of the train into eastern blackness and a now far-off valley, as if seeking advice from a distant dawn.

CHAPTER TWO

DOG

OF THE DOGS OF THE OLD PLAINS
AND OF BUILDING A TRAVOIS

TO TRAVEL properly by foot and dog I had first to learn something of the origin and nature of the old Plains dogs. Dogs became man's first animal companions many thousands of years ago. We know their origin was the wolf, but no one knows where, when, how often, or in how many different places domestication occurred.

However, we have a good idea of how domestication came about. Wolves and humans share similar hierarchical social instincts and both species run in packs. This made it possible for people to present themselves as top of the pack hierarchy to stolen or foster wolf cubs and to become acknowledged by these orphans as the alpha dog, the pack leader—the "top dog," as we still say today of a dominant human. When the adopted cubs matured and bred, people destroyed those puppies with unfavorable traits and saved those with useful characteristics or dispositions and by this means gradually developed the various dog races.

Like all animals, dogs have become stupider through domestication; the cranial capacity of a dog is measurably smaller than that of a comparably sized wolf. Yet intelligence can be overrated. It is no more likely to be an evolutionary advantage than is a longer tail, so dull-brained *Canis familiaris* now runs where *Canis lupus* never trod, and in far greater numbers.

We intuitively think of domestication as a human success story, a remarkable early achievement in human prehistory, and, to be fair to ourselves, it is. But it is equally logical to view this first of all the domestications as a clever canine adaptation to changing, human-dominated environments. The similar hunting styles and objectives of wolves and humans made domestication, from the wolf's point of view, a profitable strategy. From the days of man's earliest big game hunts wolves would have found it lucrative to associate with man to dispute the kills and to clean up the scraps and the surplus. Canines are taking a risk by cohabiting with man, for should modern human population numbers collapse, dog numbers would suffer too. But then wolves would re-expand their territories, some domestic dogs would skillfully turn feral, and the canine insurance policy of maintaining both a wild and a domestic stock of genes would prove its worth.

In North America fossil domestic dog bones date back nine thousand years. No one knows whether dogs were brought to the New World by peoples migrating from Asia or whether dogs were independently domesticated in the Americas. But it is clear that the wolf/dog division was flexible in the New World. On the Plains there were numerous observations of wolf-to-dog matings. The narrative of a German nobleman who travelled extensively on the Plains in the early 1830s, Prince Maximilian von Wied, testifies to the dynamism and fluidity of the buffalo-wolf-dog-Indian interrelationships of that time. Describing an encampment of the Sioux, Maximilian related how a circle of free-running dogs was in constant scrappy motion around and beyond the tepees. The dogs were in their turn ringed by a loose pack of wolves, who at times would "approach the Indian huts, even in the day time, and mix with the dogs." Beyond the wolves were the buffalo, upon which all else depended. When the buffalo moved on, the triple ring of predators—Indians, dogs, and wolves—followed. With such close and frequent interaction between wolf, dog, and man, it is easy to imagine how wolves were first domesticated as they approached encampments many millennia ago. Not only were there continued injections of wolf blood into the Plains dog stock, but the process worked in reverse as well. Female wolves sometimes pursued the attentions of male dogs and, as fur trader Alexander Henry related in the Red River Valley in 1801, sometimes got more than they bargained for: "The female wolves prefer our dogs to their own species, and daily come near the fort to entice the dogs. They often succeed, and if the dogs ever return, they are in a miserable condition, lean and covered with sores. Some of my men have amused themselves by watching their motions in the act of copulating; rushing upon them with an ax or club, when the dog, apprehending no danger, would remain quiet, and the wolf, unable to run off, could be dispatched."

By blood and by lifestyle Plains dogs were a tough bunch. Several early traders and explorers commented on their fierceness. Paul Kane, prairie painter and adventurer, described the Cree dogs he saw in 1846 around Fort Garry (modern Winnipeg): "These dogs are very like wolves, both in appearance and disposition, and, no doubt, [are] a cross breed between the wolf and the dog. A great many of them acknowledge no particular master and are sometimes dangerous in times of scarcity. I have myself known them to attack the horses and eat them."

Two years later Kane witnessed further dog troubles around Fort Edmonton: "The dogs generally used are of a breed peculiar to the country and partake of the character and disposition of the wolf, which they so often resemble in appearance as sometimes to have been shot in mistake. Their ferocity is so great that they are often dangerous . . . Mr. Rundell was himself attacked one evening, while walking a short distance from the fort, by a band of these brutes, belonging to the establishment."

The unfortunate Mr. Rundell was able to escape only with assistance. To the south of the prairie regions travelled by Kane, the hunter Joseph Batty visited the Crow nation and remarked: "There are no pure blooded dogs, nearly all being crossed with the wolf. In the Winter they are disconsolate, half starved looking creatures, but during the buffalo season they fare sumptuously and become very fat. These dogs fight savagely." In 1851 the Swiss adventurer Rudolph Kurz, writing in his Plains journal, agreed: "Indian dogs differ very slightly from wolves, howl like them, do not bark, and not infrequently mate with them."

You might well think that such aggressive dogs would be useful in hunting, but in practice Plains dogs were far too unruly for stalking, pointing, or retrieving. They were sometimes useful as camp watchdogs at night, creating an awful din at the approach of a stranger, but they were not dependable in this role. Although Sioux dogs had the best reputation as watchdogs, even they would sometimes ignore horse thieves making a bold night raid.

At least dogs can be eaten. Dogs were the main dish in the Dog Feast of the Plains Cree, while the Gros Ventre, Sioux, and Assiniboine also considered dog a great delicacy. Yet the Blackfoot never consumed dog meat, and some other Indian nations might only do so under starvation conditions. In other aspects of dog management there was also great diversity of practice among the New World peoples. There are reports of how some Inuit strangled dogs into unconsciousness and then smashed their incisors to prevent them from chewing on sealskin sled lines, while the fur trader Daniel Harmon reported how very kind Indians west of the Rockies were to their dogs. There he met people who spoke of their dogs as sons or daughters, and who lamented canine deaths with great anguish. The heterogeneity of New World peoples' views about dogs was paralleled among the Europeans of the time, some of whom were kind to their dogs while others, as Henry recorded, would beat their dogs to death.

Whether managed by threat or reward, the primary use of dogs on the Plains was as beasts of burden. For this reason the Hidatsa, for example, preferred big dogs, but those puppies or dogs that bit or snapped at their owners or fought too much with the other dogs were destroyed. This kind of common sense breeding management over the centuries ensured that Plains dogs were fit for the work intended.

In wooded country dogs sometimes carried side packs, but on the Plains the wood and skin travois was employed. Travois varied in design detail, but all had a basic A-frame shape made by cutting down two thin, straight tree trunks, debarking them, and lashing them together with sinew at their narrower ends. About two-thirds of the way down from the apex to the feet of the A-frame several cross-bars were tied down parallel to each other. Four or five of these together formed the load-bearing rack. Stood vertically the A-frame was about two and a half metres high and about one metre across at the base. When harnessed, the apex of the A-frame rested on the dog's back. The foot ends of the travois dragged behind the dog, sliding over mud, grass, or stones, with the natural spring of the wood cushioning the bumps. A dog could pull more weight by travois than in side packs and it was much easier to transport bulky items like wood or buffalo meat by travois than by pack.

The first Europeans to see and describe the travois were the Spaniards in 1541 on Francisco Coronado's expedition in the southern Plains. As everywhere in the New World, the Spanish were looking for gold, and for Coronado and his men the sight of an unruly train of dogs with travois provided some much-needed light entertainment during what was, in the business sense, a disappointing venture. Dog and travois were subsequently seen and described by many European explorers and traders until the horse became widespread over the Plains and supplanted the dog as a beast of burden. However, there were always a few horse-poor nations, and even horse-poor individuals in tribes where horses were abundant, who kept the dog travois tradition alive late into the nineteenth century. Even those peoples rich in horses occasionally found dogs useful when the snow was too deep for horses but crusted enough to support dogs. In 1858 geologist Henry Hind encountered a group of Cree with an extensive train of dog and travois in the Qu'Appelle Valley, and the Cree continued to use dog travois extensively into the 1860s.

While I found plenty of accounts of travois encounters, there was little written about travois construction. Made of wood, skin, and sinew, travois perish quickly in the normal course of events. I studied photographs of old travois from the Smithsonian Institution in Washington and visited Wanaskewin, a Native Canadian heritage park near Saskatoon, where several travois had been constructed for educational purposes. This all helped a little, but most valuable was the discovery of a detailed description of how to build a dog travois. In the early twentieth century an American anthropologist, Gilbert Wilson, interviewed an aged Hidatsa, Buffalo-bird-woman, on many aspects of the Hidatsa way of life around the Missouri River. Among the many things carefully described by Buffalo-bird-woman, as she remembered them from her mid-nineteenth-century childhood, were the design and construction of a dog travois. Her instructions became the model for my construction.

Having settled on a travois design, I turned to the critical problem of finding the right dog for travois work. The original Plains dogs have long since disappeared, their bloodlines not truly extirpated but hopelessly mixed with that of European breeds. New World and Old World dog-meets-dog encounters must have taken place almost as soon as parallel human encounters. In 1577 the Arctic Inuit demonstrated sled-dog training to explorer Martin Frobisher with the Englishman's own ship's dogs. By 1820, referring to the Indians of the northern Plains, Harmon wrote: "They now have a large breed among them which were brought into their country from Newfoundland, by the English, when they first established themselves on Hudson's Bay; and from that place they have been spread into every part of the country east of the Rocky Mountain."

Although there were no true Plains dogs left (frankly they seemed a bit rough to work with anyway), I still needed a dog that was similar in strength and toughness. I also needed a dog used to pulling loads from puppyhood on; it would be useless to try to train a dog that had lived its life as a pet. After careful thought I decided that a modern sled-dog husky would be the best choice. Huskies are tough outdoor survivors, the mongrel descendants of the various big dogs brought north to haul miners' gear in the gold rush days of Alaska and the Klondike. Newfoundlands, German shepherds, collies, St. Bernards, and various hounds—all were brought north and interbred with the indigenous malamutes, samoyeds, and Eskimo dogs (and also with the heavy-furred "Siberian husky," now a registered pure-bred). Out of this melting pot emerged a high-endurance, trainable dog with a strong pack hierarchy known as the "Alaskan husky," or more simply as the "husky." Its characteristics made the husky a close match to the old Plains dogs.

Many huskies are kept as house pets and would be of no use on the trail. Of those that race for their living, most run fast short-course races. What I needed was a husky adapted to longer, slower work, and with a lighter fur coat so that it would not be too prone to overheating. There is, I discovered, a subclass of short-haired huskies used for long distance and multi-day races. About one full year after my moonlit train journey through the Qu'Appelle Valley, I set out to find them.

SLED-DOG OWNERS, I learned, are themselves a breed apart, totally devoted to their dogs and their sport. Revelling in cold and feats of endurance, they complain of lengthy summers and are forever moving farther north in search of better snow conditions. To be a competitive racer you need to maintain a pack of at least thirty to forty adult dogs. Feeding and caring for so many dogs and, especially, training them, is a full-time occupation. Running sled for hours with the dogs on cold winter nights has inevitable consequences; a hot brain core enveloped in frozen cortex cells creates a special type of visionary. Generally the young dogs are named only after initial training, after which time their aptitudes, or lack of same, are known. Monikers like "Trigger," "Grumpy," or "Hammerhead" therefore reveal something of the animal's true nature. In similar fashion owners are rebaptized by the racing fraternity: "Mad Dog McIver" is a typical example. As the truly happy in this world are those obsessed (be it by golf, politics, or Russian literature), the dog handlers I met were cheerful people.

Since my travois project involved dogs, since it was quixotic in nature, and since its main object was the journey itself, it appealed to dog handlers. These were people who understood that the meaning of life is the living of it and that the point of travel is not where you are going but how you get there. It was June, from a sled-dog handler's point of view the off-season, and a good time to put my ideas forward. After a few inquiries I found myself trading thoughts with Frank Mymryk in Butler's fish and chip shop on the west shore of Last Mountain Lake, Saskatchewan. Around us the walls were covered with old photographs of the rail age, a time when frequent day trains and "moonlighters" carried people to the lake en masse. Black-and-white photos taken even yesterday can give an impression of places and times impossibly distant, yet it was only a few decades since these pictured trains were the primary means of transportation on the prairies. By necessity tourism then was concentrated, populous, and public, a healthy antidote to the solitude of the prairies which the dispersion of travel brought by the motor car only accentuates.

After a last look at the site of vanished rail platforms we set off to visit Frank's dogs. It was the first time I had seen a pack of huskies. The dogs were staked and chained just out of reach of each other. Their wild howlings and lunging at the stake made it obvious why this measure was necessary, but it was unclear to me whether their intense, feverish eyes showed affection or anger. Frank, of course, was not concerned and soon we were experimenting with broom and shovel handles tied to a husky's back in rough simulation of a travois. The dog, uncertain of what was expected of him, whined and looked confused. As we stepped slowly forward Frank's brow was furrowed. "It just might work," he finally ventured, "but not with these dogs." His animals would be, he thought, too difficult to retrain to travois. As we returned from our test walk the watching pack howled and snarled, a few dogs hiding from my eyes. Frank considered who might have suitable animals and suggested a second handler near Crooked Lake, eastward down the Qu'Appelle Valley. Driving away, I wondered how anyone was able to train these animals to do anything; they had seemed a frenzied lot.

The Crooked Lake handler was equally helpful and interested, but had few dogs. He recommended a third handler to the north of the valley, near Yorkton. There I met Jim and Elaine Tomkins a few days later. Keen racers, they managed a large pack of distance dogs. They listened carefully to my plans and then explained some of the basics of husky training and management. We watched videos of the famous Iditarod multi-day sled race across Alaska, the ambition of every red-blooded handler. Finally I was introduced to the dogs. The variety of physiques was astounding—some dogs showed hound blood, others German shepherd, while some with the northern blue ice eyes looked and acted too wild for comfort. The dogs took little exercise in the full heat of June, but by September they would be out early mornings. In teams of about eight they would run seven or eight kilometres a day, pulling a farm truck across summerfallow and stubble.

Jim introduced me to Serge, one of his most valuable animals. At eight years old he was mature and calmer than most of his fellows. By muzzle shape, by colour, and by coat texture he clearly had German shepherd in his ancestry. As a superior lead dog, that is, as the dog at the head of a harnessed team, he had proven himself intelligent and trainable. Jim and Elaine would not need Serge over the summer, but there were risks involved in loaning him out to me, from foot damage, to escape, to my overfeeding a racing-weight animal athlete. Jim and Elaine seemed unconcerned. I was given a few training aids, custom dog food, and a final reminder not to overfeed my charge. "If your travois idea will work with any dog, it will work with Serge," remarked Jim, as we pushed twenty-five kilograms of dog into my borrowed truck. I was both grateful and nervous that I was being entrusted with such a valuable animal on a handshake; Serge, on the other hand, seemed unconcerned. Well used to travel, he quickly curled asleep in the back of the truck on the return journey into the Qu'Appelle Valley.

The slopes around Katepwa Lake, where I had rented a cottage for the summer, were ideal terrain for training. As the valley runs west to east, the valley slopes generally face north or south. South-facing slopes tend to be dried out by the sun, while the cooler and damper north-facing slopes tend to be too thick with bush to allow travois travel. At Katepwa Lake the valley bends briefly to the south such that the slopes there face roughly east or west. Behind my hillside cottage the slopes faced west by southwest and thereby offered a good mix of terrain and vegetation, from cacti and shortgrass on the exposed ridges to bush and trees in the most sheltered hollows. The cottage was also close to the downstream end of Katepwa Lake. This meant it would be easy to train in the valley beyond Katepwa, out of sight and mind of the populated cottage area. "Katepwa"—say it slowly and your mouth ends in an "ah" of wonder at the beauty of the lake—is a mellifluous word derived from the language of the Cree. Like the French "Qu'Appelle" it means, in English, "Who calls?" It is a reference to the echoes you sometimes hear in the valley and coulee hills and a reference, too, to the calling Spirit said by the First Peoples to wander the valley lakes.

It was in the wooded slopes and damp sheltered hollows that I searched for the raw materials to build my travois. According to the records, aspen poplar was the proper wood to use. Humble aspen! It is the commonest and also the most audible tree on the prairies. Wisely the aspen sets its little rounded leaves at the end of long flattened stalks so they can swing freely in the lightest of breezes. This design limits the chance of being blown down in a prairie gale and is an arboreal parallel to the willingness of the prairie grasses to acquiesce to the sovereignty of the prairie wind. Aspen leaves murmur on, wistful and plaintive, when other trees fall silent, making this poplar as easy to identify by ear as by eye. Long ago in Europe the Romans were drawn by the whispering leaves to hold public meetings under black-scarred white boughs. At times I too have listened long to the leaves.

Nonetheless, during my search for raw materials aspen audibility was a side issue; I rued their devilishly twisted trunks as I rejected tree after crooked tree. A straight trunk, and in particular one that did not thin out quickly from the base, was only to be found in the densest possible stand, where trees shot straight upwards, fighting for the light, their spindly trunks well protected from windthrow by the mass of their companions around them. There was no room to swing a hatchet in such tight quarters and I would have been better off with a saw, but I had determined to use only three ancient tools for travois construction: a hatchet, a knife, and a needle. The steel versions I employed were modern to be sure, but all three had their direct pre-European stone or bone antecedents that often took an edge as sharp as steel does today.

Slowly I chipped my way through two trunks, my half-strokes angled from above. It then took a long time to work the young trees to the ground, for their branches grabbed and snagged on their fellows at every opportunity. But eventually persistence was rewarded and I could start trimming the trunks before then working them free of the bush. All the while mosquitoes answered the call of sweat and heavy breathing. This was a glimpse of the trials to come.

By evening I considered a good day's work complete. I believed, too, that I had left a corner of valley bush in better shape than when I had found it; the surrounding trees would quickly fill in the two small gaps I had left and would be all the more vigorous given the unexpected gift of extra space and light. Many of the aspen and mixed wood stands in the valley and its coulees, no longer regenerated by cleansing prairie fires, are unnaturally old and dense. Aspen, like many prairie plants, thrives under fire conditions, quickly sending up new suckers after a burn. But now the trees grow overmature, their heartwood turns soft and punky, and they die a vertical death of disease and old age rather than re-emerging phoenix-like from flame and ash.

The next day I slowly stripped the bark with my knife, hefting the wood from hand to hand, coming to know each knot and burr intimately. The smell of wood was rich and pungent, the colors clear, the feel still slick with the sap of life. The two travois poles that emerged from underneath the bark next had to be bound to form the apex of the A-frame. I considered carefully which should be bound atop the other, sighting the line of the poles and testing for any bias in the wood's natural resilience and spring. Finally I committed, incised a groove near the end of what would be the lower pole, and slotted in the upper pole. This union was lashed with tight-bound sinew. I then debarked the cross-poles that would form the load rack and cut grooves for them in the new travois shafts. I turned each cross-pole carefully in its grooves, testing for the best fit, before binding them down.

Around the apex of the travois I stitched animal skins, for as the apex rode directly on the dog's back it had to be cushioned to prevent chafing and burring. The skins also served as an anchor for leather loops to which the chest belt and cinch strap would be attached. Buffalo-bird-woman used buffalo hide for the apex fur, but, not having any buffalo to hand, I decided to try rabbit skins. The long strips needed for load straps I cut from cow leather. I also cut a broad chest belt to allow for a strong, even pull without the belt digging into the dog's chest.

I was inexperienced at wood or leatherwork and so progressed embarrassingly slowly. Every stage of construction was a small adventure. How few of us now know the satisfaction of working with natural materials, with wood and skin and sinew, each still alive in the hand! I felt, when my odd conveyance was complete, deeply grateful for the privilege of experiencing travois construction.

It was time now to teach an old dog new tricks. As a sled dog Serge had been trained to work in a team, not on his own, and he was used to receiving direction from behind, not from in front. Most basically, for Serge, to work meant to run. Racing huskies almost never walk; their life alternates between running and being staked out. So I started training by simply walking Serge on a lead. This commonplace idea was a new experience for him and it took a few days before he was comfortable with the idea of walking rather than running. And not before time; for my own survival I alternated the leash from right to left hand frequently, but even so my arm sockets were stretched and challenged till the muscle fibers flared with heat. Serge had a haughty disregard for any other dogs we might come across; he seemed to think all other canines beneath his notice. Free-running dogs in turn gave him a wide berth and then sometimes followed after him at a safe distance, sniffing vigorously at his unfamiliar and clearly worrying scent.

On one walk there was an amusing break in Serge's standoffishness when a puppy unexpectedly ran up from the lakeshore and began jumping at Serge's face. In his study of dog behavior scientist-philosopher Konrad Lorenz observed how even the most aggressive male dog is psychologically programmed to be gentle to puppies. Here was Serge, the noble lead dog, able to order and discipline all challengers in his unruly home pack, reduced to the status of an embarrassed grandfather uncertain of what to do with an over-affectionate grandchild. Serge looked up at me with a clearly pained expression and the unspoken request that we move on from this disconcerting situation, which we duly did.

Occasionally on these walks strangers stopped to compliment me on "my" fine dog, and I felt a completely unearned glow of satisfaction. More often than not people mistook Serge for a female. This was probably because of his gold, black, and white face markings, for in some breeds a tricolour patterning is characteristic of females and many people are aware of this subconsciously.

The critical training moment came in early July when I hitched the travois to Serge for the first time. For days I had worried how he would react. He stood patiently while I harnessed him to travois, but then froze, unwilling to move with this strange contraption shackled to his back. One step at a time, I coaxed him forward. What most unnerved him was the scratching sound of the dragging travois ends over stones or rough ground. On thick grass, where the travois was next to silent, he was much more relaxed. Yet after a few days Serge was comfortable with the travois even crossing a surface as noisy as gravel.

I began adding weights to the load rack. The old Plains traders disagreed as to how much weight travois dogs could pull. There are a few accounts of dogs pulling up to forty-five kilograms or more, but many eyewitnesses reported much lighter loads. Serge was eventually able to pull up to twenty-seven kilograms over short distances, but for day trekking over rough country a load of ten to thirteen kilograms seemed about right.

I had wondered how I would encourage Serge to follow on behind me, free of any lead or tie, but from the very first trial he followed naturally. The disadvantage of this arrangement was that I might not immediately notice if Serge got stuck or decided to chase after some game trail. But having Serge walk freely behind made for a quieter walk for me, allowed Serge to choose his own route through scrub or across slope, and meant that Serge was not kicking up clouds of mosquitoes in front of me.

Soon we were trekking boldly up and down the hills behind the cottage and exploring the nature and limits of dog and travois travel. I pointed out to Serge that you could not move backwards with a travois and that I did not appreciate having to disentangle him after he plunged enthusiastically downslope into the bush in pursuit of some deer trail, only to end up hopelessly wedged in the deepest of thickets. Serge was puzzled the first time this happened, ashamed the second, and there was no third. Serge himself figured out that tacking upslope was the easiest way to bring a travois load to the top of a hill, and he taught himself to tack downslope as well, after another early miscalculation. Initially he tried to go straight downhill under load, but the travois slid forward over his head and sent him skidding downslope on his rear end, his face wrinkled with pained embarrassment.

Gradually we ventured farther afield for training. I soon learned to avoid places where there were many people about. Of those we met while working with travois, rural folk commented favourably, but city people were sometimes deeply suspicious. In the cities most people have forgotten the concept of working dogs entirely and for many urbanites the idea of making a "pet" work is abhorrent. After one unhappy encounter I half expected to be reported to the Society for the Prevention of Cruelty to Animals. There was no consistency to the urban view, for no one objected to horse riding, although sitting upon an animal after sticking a steel bit through its mouth must objectively rate as a far greater imposition than hitching said animal to a travois. Nonetheless, I was challenging custom and expectations and, as Kurz sagely noted in an 1851 journal entry about Indian dogs as draft animals: "There are certain philanthropists . . . who in their zeal for dogs' welfare give them a higher place in their esteem than they ascribe to man, of whom they exact any and every sort of work."

I took to rising about dawn and setting off directly for a few hours' training. Originally the early start was to avoid the hot sun of July, but soon the beauty of the morning itself seemed reason enough. Serge was always eager to go; belying his age he would gambol and kick up his heels for joy like a young calf in spring. After two or three hours' training we would reward ourselves with a rest by the Qu'Appelle River. I would go for a swim while Serge would hunt the banks. By the time we returned to the cottage I had a well-earned appetite for breakfast. Never have I felt so fit and healthy as from that simple daily regime.

A training walk with Serge and mosquitoes

We frequented one coulee in particular. It was typical of many Qu'Appelle tributaries and lay not far east of the end of the lake. Hiking this coulee you could almost forget the presence of man in the landscape, except for three unfortunate reminders. The first was a fence line, running remorselessly between two cardinal points, oblivious to the natural coulee curves. The second was the earth-scar of a buried gas pipeline that ran in a startlingly straight line down one steep side of the coulee and up the other. The third was an old farm dump, a full assortment of garbage tipped down the coulee side and piling up and into the bush along the bottom. The dry prairie climate had preserved even the paper content of the long-abandoned tip. Each spring the garbage would creep with the snowmelt a little deeper into the bush and a little closer to the coulee creek bed.

Occasionally I caught glimpses of the primeval hunter in Serge. Once, as I was emerging from a river swim, I saw him at river's edge downstream, lunging for a killdeer too dim-witted to fly off. As Serge's jaws snapped shut the plover's shrill cries were extinguished, replaced by the popping of bird bones audible at fifty metres. I felt a pang of guilt at my poor guardianship, especially as the killing appeared to be pointless, for Serge made no effort to eat his prey. Instead, uncertain of what to do with it, he dropped it into the river, where it spun and floated away, a little mass of crumpled bones and feathers. Another day Serge took great pleasure in savaging a dead jackrabbit he found along the trail.

As our training routine continued, Serge grew in my esteem. He was teaching me more about travois travel than I could possibly suggest to him. He became a full partner, rather than a pupil in need of instruction. If he slowed or deviated from the trail behind me, it was for some good reason, if only I was clever enough to see it. I felt increasingly humbled by the unquestioning trust he put in me, following me faithfully, and without complaint, through bush, ravine, or wetland (although he drew the line at rivers—but more about that later). In Britain you see sheep driven by their shepherd from behind, as Serge had been driven as a sled dog. But in southern Africa the shepherd leads and the sheep follow of their own volition, trusting in his judgment, as Serge now trusted in mine. I had no doubt that my growing faith in Serge was justified, but I was not sure his faith in me was half so deserved. The journey to come would surely test it.

CHAPTER THREE

"MUSH!"

OF PRAIRIE JOURNEYS THROUGH HEAT, SNOW,
& MOSQUITOES WITH A REMARKABLE HUSKY

IT WAS a cloudy, calm early morning in mid-July, heavy with humidity, when man and dog stood face to face. "Mush!" I called, keen to mark the commencement of our travois odyssey with dignity and resonance. Serge remained motionless and gazed at me with his eyes wrinkled round with puzzlement. I tried again with a rising inflection, "Come on!" and he stepped forward. In truth, modern sled-dog handlers rarely call "Mush!" to start their team; "Hike!" is most often heard. But the historical romance of "mush," from the French *marchons* ("Let's go"), appealed to me, if not to Serge. Our journey's starting point was the north side of Katepwa Lake, a mile from the eastern end of the lake. Our destination was the confluence of the Qu'Appelle and Assiniboine Rivers in Manitoba, some 225 kilometres by foot down-valley to the east. It was my intention to follow the general line of the valley but, as conditions permitted, to travel through all types of terrain: the valley bottomlands, the slopes, and the valley edge and toplands. The key constraining factor was our need to remain reasonably close to the river, our source of water. Serge was pulling all his own food, a bit of mine, and a tent. It amounted to a twelve kilogram load, plus travois. I was travelling reasonably light as well, carrying perhaps eighteen kilograms in my backpack.

From just beyond the end of Katepwa Lake we followed a dirt trail through the bottomlands for four or five kilometres, at one point crossing a bridge onto the south side of the river. Then we turned off across scrub grazing land. The reality of prairie travel was already all around us and, may God be my witness on that muggy valley morning, it was a mosquito misery beyond anything I had ever experienced. Nor was I a mosquito novice; years earlier, while stranded in the wilds of Labrador, I had kept up my spirits with dark-humoured estimations of blood loss and survival time for an unprotected human exposed to the ravages of the local mosquito population. But this morning in the valley, speculation was overwhelmed by reality; there was nothing abstract about my calculations when I termed the collective that swarmed about me in ravenous insatiability an "insanity" of mosquitoes.

The power of shame alone stopped me from turning back so early in the trek, yet I could not visualize surviving this exposure long term. It was many days later that I discovered that we had been travelling through a freak mosquito population explosion that was breaking all records in prairie Manitoba and Saskatchewan. Mosquito trap counts over five times higher than any previously recorded were astonishing observers, so in retrospect my despondency was forgivable. In happy contrast to myself, Serge was untroubled by mosquitoes, except around his muzzle and eyes. For Serge a bit of bear grease, if I had had any, would have been the traditional protection for these exposed hairless points.

Mosquitoes, like the biblical poor, have always been with us. Huron and Iroquois creation traditions tell of a dualistic struggle between twin brothers: the evil brother created mosquitoes as big as turkeys; the good brother could not destroy them but reduced them to their present size. The Plains Indians used the traditional mosquito protections of smoke and wind and sometimes rubbed sage on the skin. Sage is not a very effective repellent, but doubtless every imaginable plant, animal, or mineral extract has been tested for possible mosquito repellency over the millennia of Indian habitation on the Plains.

In July of 1754 one of the very first Europeans in the prairies, Anthony Hendry, complained near the mouth of the Saskatchewan River: "The Musketoes are now intolerable, giving us neither peace day nor night." Mosquitoes figure in almost every Plains trader's journal that followed. In July of 1806 Alexander

Henry and his party were riding north of the Assiniboine River with, he wrote, "the mosquitoes tormenting us as usual. Our horses, which had little rest last night, were almost ungovernable, tearing up the grass, throwing their fore feet over their heads to drive away the insects, and biting their sides till our legs were in danger of their teeth. In a word the poor tortured and enraged beasts often attempted to throw themselves down and roll in the water. We also suffered intolerably, being almost prevented from taking breath."

In August of 1858 Henry Hind described trying to bribe his way to some bush fruit near the South Saskatchewan River: "I offered the Cree guide a piece of tobacco for a tin cup full of raspberries, he tried to win it, but after a short struggle with these terrible insects he rushed from the hill side and buried his face in the smoke of the fire we had lit in the hope of expelling them from the neighbourhood of our camp; the horses became quite frantic under the attacks of their tormentors, holding their heads over the smoke, and crowding together in a vain endeavour to avoid the clouds of insatiable insects which surrounded us. Both man and beast passed a miserable, restless, and sleepless night." Hind recorded that in the Plains south of their settlement the Red River Métis particularly feared capture by hostile Sioux, whose favorite summer tortures included, he said, staking out a prisoner naked at the edge of a marsh, there to die of exposure, tormented by thirst and mosquitoes.

By the early twentieth century some travellers were taking a more scientific, quantitative, approach to mosquitoes. Ernest Thompson Seton, the master naturalist of Manitoba, devoted a full chapter to the blood eaters in his account of his 1907 journeys in the "arctic prairies." Some evenings he counted the numbers of mosquitoes resting on a small area of tent canvas and then extrapolated to the entire tent surface, once calculating 24,000 mosquitoes on the tent. He estimated as many again flying just outside the door. Desperate for repellents, he experimented with frog secretions and with fungal juice from manure piles. Nothing worked. Yet he nonetheless predicted, with all the misplaced confidence of his time, that "it is certain that knowledge will confer on man the power to wipe them out."

We now live in a skeptical age and the resourcefulness of mosquitoes justifies pessimism. Although mosquito larvae need water, the eggs can survive for years under dry conditions, so egg-bearing females seek out by smell not only where water is now, but also the dried-out low spots to which water will return. In their search for the rich warm blood they need for egg production, female mosquitoes can follow a carbon dioxide exhalation trail for tens of metres, and then home in on body scent and heat. Their sensitivity to blood temperature variations is so refined that surrounding oneself with sacrificial children (who normally have a slightly higher body temperature than adults) is one of the best defences for the adult human. You might reasonably think that, as "the naked ape," humans must feature highly in any mosquito's vision of paradise; we are huge slow-moving masses of liquid protein pulsing under a thin skin. In reality, though this is often hard to believe, most mosquito species prefer the blood of other animals to the blood of humans—birds are a common target. We are in fact often bitten for lack of a better alternative.

The eighteen or so mosquito species native to the Canadian prairies fall into two categories. The masticators feed by tearing open the skin with their mouthparts and then licking up the pooling blood. The drillers feed more elegantly by knifing a slender pipette through the skin and directly into a blood vessel; positive blood pressure then forces blood up the pipette. This difference in feeding technique explains why some mosquitoes (the drillers) can "bite" through a tightly woven shirt, while others (the masticators) cannot.

To combat the vision of days of perdition ahead of me, I tried to concentrate on the moment, claiming each hundred metres' progress as a personal victory in tenacity. On our left we were soon passing alongside Skinner's Marsh, an important habitat for ducks, coots, waders, grebes, and geese. Seen at sunrise or sunset, the marsh is beautiful, aglow with rich reflected colours, as the contented cackling of ducks soothes the spirit. But through this morning's haze the marsh looked a sickly, fetid place. It had been engineered in part by Ducks Unlimited, an organization whose chief purpose is the production of wildfowl for hunters and the extent of whose financial resources and influence is only dimly surmised by most prairie dwellers. At the moment I resented DU (as they like to be known) not for their slick sunset-over-the-productive-marshlands marketing but for the boost to the local mosquito population that was a by-product, however unintended, of wetlands construction. This summer I reckoned that the biomass of mosquito production exceeded that of waterfowl.

Beyond the marsh lay the first serious physical barrier, Redfox Creek, a coulee channel tributary to the Qu'Appelle that wound back some forty kilometres southward from the valley. The creek itself was hidden to the eye, but what I could see was a dark-hued ribbon of vegetation running across the valley from the south to meet the river at the foot of the north-slope hills. As we approached, the greenery seemed to close together and thicken, threatening impenetrability. At the edge of the bush I tied Serge to a tree and then slid into the tangle in search of a route through. Cautiously I worked through the lattice of growth to reach the lip of the concealed stream channel. The channel was dry, but sharply incised some four metres deep into the valley alluvium. Beyond it was another web of interlaced brushwork. I returned to Serge, unhitched and shouldered his travois, and penetrated back to the edge of the channel. I scrambled down the near-vertical wall and then picked my way along the bottom, clambering over the spring flood debris that littered the floor, until I found what looked like a promising route up into the far-side bush. From there I slowly worked forward to finally emerge victorious into grassland. Dropping the travois, I turned and repeated the round-trip journey twice more to get our packs through. Serge I released to pursue scent trails up and down the channel floor. When I emerged from the bush for the last time, my sweat, heat, and carbon dioxide trail had gathered me the affections of thousands of mosquitoes; the heavy humid air seemed to reflect and magnify their humming into a dull roar that throbbed deep into my brain.

Across a fence line ahead of us lay a large pasture with unknown far boundaries and without visible occupants. The grass stretched away dry and well grazed. I entered cautiously, on the lookout for cattle or horses. But the pasture was quiet, and without fresh droppings. It was only when we came over a low rise that I saw a vast herd of grazing cattle, hundreds of metres distant, ahead of us and to the left. We could try to squeeze through unnoticed close to the hills on the right, or we could make a long retreat. Keeping one eye out for a possible bull and a second eye fixed on the nearest fence line in case rapid retreat became advisable, I stepped forward, bearing right, trying to appear inconspicuous or, failing that, at least innocuous.

The apostles Matthew and Luke both recount the story of Jesus telling his disciples that the Lord marked even such seemingly trivial events as the fall of a sparrow. To writer Wallace Stegner this could nowhere be more true than on the prairies. In that unforgiving landscape the simple act of standing upright was, he believed, a challenge to anonymity; the body vertical was like an exclamation mark demanding notice from God in "a land to mark the sparrow's fall." On this day we found it no more possible to elude one dumb cow's notice than it would be for a sparrow to escape the Lord's Plains omniscience. No sooner had one bovine detected our movement than the entire animal mass was stumbling forward. Dust and noise rose together as panic rippled forward, and a vast prairie rumble of motion rolled on far ahead of us. It was an echo of the great buffalo stampedes of Plains past, for in the same peculiar manner as the buffalo herds, these cattle moved toward and across our path, even as they moved away from us. I cursed their obtuse panic and fervently hoped there was no rancher nearby, justifiably angered by our cattle-rousing trespass. Serge, for his part, was completely unmoved by the spectacle.

Eventually the cattle shambled out of view in the far distance. I continued on cautiously, uncomfortably conspicuous in a pasture that stretched beyond the horizon, while Serge walked unconcerned. The cattle never again reappeared, although a trail of raised dust hung heavy in the dead air and marked their passage clearly. It took nearly an hour's walking before we reached and crossed a second fence line and so definitively put dust and cattle behind us. Ahead, however, was another complication. Through my pocket binoculars I could make out a small posse of horses perhaps two kilometres distant. If we were an annoyance for cattle, horses could be a danger for us, for horses instinctively dislike unfamiliar dogs. Serge was doubly vulnerable, for he had no experience of horses that I knew of and his mobility was greatly restricted by the travois. We had to be wary if he was not to end up with a kicked-in skull. Through the binoculars I followed the relevant lines of fencing and concluded that the horses were safely in a separate pasture. Reassured, I proceeded, nonetheless sticking close to a fence line on our left in case of trouble. My plan was to follow this fence until it joined the cross-fence separating us from the horses ahead and then to walk along the cross-fence line, bearing right and southward toward the valley slopes, with the intention of getting around the horse pasture via the slopes if necessary.

Sure enough the horses soon noticed our presence and began trotting, then cantering, along the cross-fence ahead of us. What I had failed to see was that at the crucial right angle juncture the fence was broken down. There was, in fact, nothing separating us from the horses. Within seconds they had rounded the broken corner and were heading toward us at a fast canter.

It was a terrible shock. Serge could not escape through the fence line on our left with his travois attached, so I rushed to release him from the harness and tossed the travois over the fence. Then I aggressively shoved Serge under the bottom wire; he was baffled by my urgency and reluctant to go. Finally I crossed through myself just as the horses arrived at speed. All parties examined each other cautiously over and through the fence, all of us relieved, I think, at the barrier between us—good fences do make good neighbours. Serge and I made a long pause for reflection. We were now confined for the moment to the left side of the fence and our only possible route forward was toward the river. We set off, again parallel to the fence, shadowed by a dozen horses, a few of which stamped their feet nervously.

The route turned steadily more soggy. Somewhere ahead of us was the Qu'Appelle River, but the flatness of the floodplain gave no clue as to how far away the nearest meander might be. The prospect of having to cross the river in the clouds, in the insanities, of mosquitoes that swarmed about us was almost too much to bear. Again I tried to focus on the moment at hand and the next few steps ahead. My immediate concern had to be to find the river without first sinking deep into a swamp. Our route through patches of marsh and slough turned and twisted as much as the unseen river itself. Distrusting their own footing, the horses on the far side of the fence abandoned their shadowing exercise and moved off somewhere to the east in their pasture.

When finally we reached the river's edge, both of us were, despite our best efforts, already soaked up to our respective thighs. Yet, crucially, the baggage was still dry and I was intent on keeping it that way. In August of 1807 Henry and his party had faced a similar problem when trying to cross the Cypress River, a tributary to the Assiniboine. Their goods were heavy, so a raft had to be built to float them safely over. Naturally the necessary raw materials were on the far side of the river. Henry wrote:

> There being no alternative, we unloaded our horses and stripped. I crossed over, collected what brush I could find, and with the poplar formed a raft so very slight as to carry scarcely more than 50 pounds' weight. The mosquitoes were intolerable, and as we were obliged to remain naked for about four hours, we suffered more than I can describe . . . Every time I landed the mosquitoes plagued me insufferably; and still worse, the horse I had crossed over upon was so tormented that he broke his fetters and ran away. I was under the cruel necessity of pursuing him on the plains entirely naked; fortunately I caught him and brought him back . . . The water in this river is always excessively cold, and by the time we got all over our bodies were as blue as indigo; we were shivering like aspen leaves, and our legs were cut and chafed by the coarse stiff grass.

With Henry's unhappy experience in mind I stripped and slid swiftly into the water to test the depth of the thirty-metre crossing. With an upturned nose, it was

Fording the River Qu'Appelle

just possible to cross on tiptoes. The problem was maintaining my balance, for the bottom was greasy mud and the current threatened to lift me up and over. I would have to be extremely careful—and lucky—to get all our gear across safe and dry.

Buffalo-bird-woman had told of how her Plains dogs would boldly swim across the Missouri at low ebb, allowing her to wade behind and keep the load dry by lifting the travois shaft ends just clear of the water. I swam back across the river and explained this idea to Serge, all the while squatting as submerged as possible to hide my nakedness from the mosquitoes. Serge was distinctly unimpressed, taking an "I am a husky, not a retriever" view of my proposal, and politely but firmly declined to be coaxed into the water, even without his travois. Northern dogs often have a phobia about open water, for falling in when the air temperature is below freezing can be fatal. Or perhaps Serge was beginning to question my leadership skills—who could have blamed him? So far this day I had consistently led us into trouble.

Whatever the reason, I had to work alone. I made three painstaking round-trip crossings, once with my pack, once with Serge's, and once with the travois. Each crossing under load was a trial in concentration and stoicism as I carefully leaned my body weight against the current, while above the waterline the mosquitoes feasted on my arms and face. That still left Serge on the wrong side of the river. The logic and implication of the whole operation had not been lost on him; he looked increasingly discomfited as our gear piled up on the opposite bank. I am sorry to say that, in view of his relative immunity to the mosquitoes and his wholehearted non-contribution to the crossing, I was not disposed to sympathy. Unfair, I know, considering neither the crossing nor the journey was Serge's idea. In any event, there was a brief struggle, and suddenly a very reluctant husky felt terra firma slip away underpaw—perhaps for all time, to judge by his expression. I towed him across by the collar without further comment from either of us.

Once out of the water I dressed with remarkable rapidity. With everything, and everybody, across without incident, there was fair cause for thankfulness, and even a grain of self-confidence. But as we set off again, picking our way through further marshy bottomlands, I was, like Henry after his crossing, "much fatigued and harassed." Worse, I was no longer thinking clearly.

When our progress was blocked by a creek flowing from north to south toward the river now to the right of us, I was uncertain where we were, although I knew we had not come as far as I had intended. But here at least there was a slight rise and a patch of dry grass, and a source of water too. In any case I felt too exhausted to undertake even this modest creek crossing and go on any farther, so I pitched tent there in the middle of the floodplain, crawled in to escape the mosquitoes, and promptly fell asleep.

Half recovered by dusk, I was just beginning to pick up my spirits, congratulating myself on the successful river crossing, when I noticed a herd of horses approaching through the twilight. I cursed my foolishness. Before pitching the tent I had seen these horses, but they had appeared distant even in binoculars, and had been on the far side of the river, so I had assumed that we would not be troubled. If I had not been so tired I would have realized it was fully possible that they might ford the river. Now it was too late. I kept Serge close to hand, ready to throw him into the tent if necessary. These were mares with foals, undoubtedly protective. At about fifty metres' distance they stopped their approach and began patrolling around the tent in a half circle bounded by the creek. They continued their nervous trampling sentry work all night, for most of which time I remained in an uneasy half-sleep. When I rose, exhausted, in the dimness of early dawn, they whinnied to each other, but still kept their distance as they watched us pack. I was relieved to leave them behind. As we waded through the creek the cold morning water drove off drowsiness and sharpened the senses for the day ahead.

The second day's terrain was much easier going, as we were following the general line of a dry-weather byroad at the foot of the north-slope hills. It was now a simple matter to wander across open pasturelands, as a quick-exit scramble to the fenced-off byroad was always possible in case of trouble. But, although we had made a dawn start, heat became a problem for Serge as the sun rose higher in a cloudless sky. Our pace slowed accordingly. Finally, after several hours' progress, Serge simply lay down limp in the grass and refused to follow me forward. Just a hundred metres ahead stood an old abandoned farmstead with the promise of shade and shelter for us both. By now Serge and I understood each other remarkably well, yet I could find no way of explaining to him the advantages of carrying on just a little farther. I stood silent on the prairie between Serge and the sun, blessing him with shade for a few minutes. The north slopes above us were dry and still with no hint of a cooling wind. When I urged Serge to move on, he turned his head away and pressed his body low against the ground, as if willing himself to sink into the cool soil below. I bent to stand him up and felt his body slump strangely flaccid in my hands. It was the classic example of passive resistance, a limp-doll act that communicated unwillingness while trying not to offend. On a December 1858 journey along the Red River, Hind's sled dogs used the same technique, taking advantage of a snowfall to feign lifelessness in hopes of avoiding sled work:

We were detained for more than three hours on one occasion after a heavy snow storm, by some of the dogs preserving perfect silence and a motionless position under their covering of snow, within thirty yards of our camp fire. They were found by dint of walking systematically round the camp fire in a continually enlarging circle, the half-breeds being quite aware of the advantage which these cunning animals would take of their accidental concealment. A loud shout every now and then announced that a searcher had stumbled over a truant, whose depressed mien and conscious look showed how well he knew that he had been the cause of anxiety and trouble.

I took on some of Serge's travois load and waited a few minutes more. Then I moved off ahead, calling him once, but not looking back. This time he followed and in short order we reached the shade of a grey-bleached wall of a clapboard farmhouse. I was grateful for this lonely marker of anonymous homestead failure, bent and desiccated by wind and sun. We rested, Serge's head down, mine up, staring at blue sky and soundless Swainson's hawks circling high above.

Before moving on I transferred still more of Serge's load into my pack. It was only a short walk farther before we reached a section of the Hudson's Bay Company's old cart trail. In the nineteenth century the company used ox carts to transport trading supplies up-valley and return with pemmican down-valley. In the latter days of the fur trade, pemmican, a high-energy, compact, and nearly imperishable foodstuff made of dried and pounded buffalo meat mixed with melted fat, was vital to fuel the traders' huge canoeist appetites on the rivers north and east of the prairies. The ox carts had here left broadly rutted depressions that captured just enough extra moisture to let the grass grow rich and thick. I unharnessed Serge, leaving him free to explore, while I sat in search of small-scale discovery, watching for mice or voles. Serge enjoyed the tall grass, partly because of its coolness and the wealth of odors its humidity harboured, but partly, too, I am certain, because of its mystery and the thrill of exploration in grass that waved above his head. In cool weather or warm, given a choice, he would often walk in the tallest grass, despite its added resistance to the travois.

The trail rolled gently over the spurs of the north slope, a ribbon of green amidst the pale, sun-cured shortgrass. We moved slowly, the land quiescent around us in the midday sun. At a north-south country road that traversed the valley, the cart trail ended. We turned briefly south along this gravel road and at the river bridge made a happy discovery. On the bridge's underside were the gourdlike mud nests of a colony of hundreds of cliff swallows whose cease-less, graceful hunting flight swept a small and precious zone free of mosqui-toes. Mosquito relief, water, shade—these basics could not have been more wel-come; the aesthetics of swallow aeronautics were a bonus. Serge and I dozed and splashed the warm late afternoon hours away in our avian sanctuary. The dome of sky arched infinitely distant, and here in midvalley the valley walls, too, were remote and aloof. As usual, the woods were thick on the north-facing slopes: poplar, elm, ash, and Manitoba maple. The sun-dried south-facing slopes, whose spurs we had been walking over, supported only shortgrasses except in a few sheltered hollows, but in two days we had already walked far enough eastward that the climate was slightly too humid to allow for the pincushion cactus that pierces paw and foot on the driest slopes around Lake Katepwa.

We pitched camp at Ellisboro crossing, not far south from the bridge. The river crossing here had been an important one during the early days of agricultur-al settlement, but had thereafter faded into obscurity. Two tiny wooden churches, one Anglican and one United, each built in the 1890s, stood face to face as testa-ment to the site's past centrality. These isolated churches were in unexpectedly pristine condition, lovingly maintained by the nearest prairie community some sixteen kilometres to the south. In each church a pot-bellied wood-burning stove with an extended flue dominated a sweet-smelling wood-furnished interior.

One explanation for the relatively high percentage of churchgoers in the United States, compared to other Western nations, including Canada, is the vibrant free market and degree of competition that exists among U.S. churches, all vying to

Camp at Ellisboro

make themselves more attractive to potential adherents. Canada, by contrast, has always been too large, its population too small, and its resources too thinly spread to allow for the free-wheeling diversity, economic and ecclesiastical, that drives the United States. The Hudson's Bay and North West fur trading companies were forced by resource scarcity to amalgamate in 1821, and the United Church (a melding of Methodists, Congregationalists, and most Presbyterians) that I saw here was itself a product of ecumenicalism driven in part by similar logistical practicalities. Here at Ellisboro I wondered if two Christian houses had not always been an overreach of optimism, or if, in an earlier time, they had both been truly needed.

At the moment I was thankful for both churches. Any building can be a psychological comfort when crossing the prairies, and to see two as fine as these was a blessing indeed. I studied the hills; they were more rounded here than those framing the lakes to the west, and in the slanting rays of the evening sun they glowed a warm auburn.

The beauty of this place has been known to man for thousands of years. From its origin in the flatlands south of the valley, Adair Coulee winds northward until its creek emerges from the valley walls near Ellisboro. Not far up from the coulee mouth are the remains of stone tools and the blackened charcoal of ancient hearths. Such evidence of early human occupation is frequent in the tributary coulees of the Qu'Appelle near their junctions with the great valley, more frequent in fact than on the valley floor itself. It is possible that Dog Age people camped as often on the valley floodplain as in the coulees and that spring flooding and sedimentation in past millennia has washed away or buried evidence of valley occupation. But people probably preferred the coulee encampments to the valley proper for security reasons, for easy access to wood, for clean spring water, and for shelter from winter wind.

I slept happily that night, content with my place in the long thin line of valley habitation. About dawn I was awake. Soon after we set off. It was sunny and calm; the temperature already 14° C. The mosquitoes were hellish, but I felt, if unhappy about this, more confident than I had been two far-off mornings ago. My plan was straightforward: to walk as far and as quickly as possible before heat again became a major problem for Serge. Full of simple focus, we advanced without incident until, after about four and a half hours, with the temperature at 23° C, Serge, without warning, collapsed behind me.

I was stunned. Serge's limp-dog act the day before had reassured me that before overheating to a danger point he would show his unwillingness or inability to continue. But today he had faithfully followed on behind me showing no sign of stress—or at least none that I could read—until collapsing from heat exhaustion. I removed the travois and dribbled precious drinking water on his head, but he was too weak to respond. As I squatted helplessly beside him, waiting, desperately hoping he would recover, my chest was tight with shame and fear.

Dogs are not well designed to cope with heat. A fur coat is one obvious disadvantage, but the most fundamental problem is body position. A body stretched out horizontally, low to the ground, is fully exposed both to the sun above and to heat radiating up from the ground below. It is akin to being trapped in a permanent sunbathing position. In addition dogs (like pigs, but unlike horses) cannot sweat and can only try to increase cooling transpiration by faster panting, which pushes moisture-absorbing air across their deliberately oversized tongues.

By contrast humans, thanks partly to our long evolution in warm landscapes, are more resistant to heat stress than we normally realize. Our vertical posture spares us the full impact of solar and ground heating and elevates us into any cooling breeze. We are largely furless, except on top of the head, where hair protects against sunburn. We can also, when acclimatized to heat, process and sweat out prodigious quantities of water to control body temperature. The Querandí Indians of the Pampas survived by exploiting our heat-tolerance advantage over fleeter, four-footed animals. Like some heat-resistant wolf pack, they relentlessly harried the Pampas deer under the midday sun until their quarry collapsed from heat exhaustion. There is good evidence, too, that in distant colder times our ancestors used a similar heat-exhaustion technique to bring down powerful animals such as the mammoth.

Had I unwittingly brought down Serge for good or in some way permanently damaged him? Time flowed painfully slowly as anxiety twisted my gut into pulsating knots. Yet after a few minutes Serge recovered enough to flex his legs and the crisis was over. A minute or two more and he was drinking water. A further pause and he looked completely recuperated. The whole incident, from collapse to apparent full recovery, had lasted less than ten minutes. I waited a while longer to let his body temperature fall further, then shouldered most of his weight load. I stood up, weak and emotionally drained, and set off cautiously. Always now I was looking back to check on Serge's progress, and we took frequent short stops, the kind dogs prefer. Nervous of damaging his health or spirit, I was eventually carrying all but a token kilogram or two of the travois load and by the time we reached a suitable campsite, it was my turn to collapse into shade. It was noon, 27° C, with a July sun on the open Plains, but owing to the cursed mosquitoes, I had had to keep well covered up.

The chosen site was a small rise north of the river. My hope was that the exposed location might be windy enough to discourage mosquitoes, but the day remained stubbornly calm. For a long time I was too hot and tired even to pitch the tent to escape the blood-hungry hordes, but underlying my fatigue was deep relief that Serge appeared none the worse for his experience. If I wrecked anyone's body, let it be my own!

Much later that afternoon we walked the few hundred yards down to the river for water. In earlier days the Qu'Appelle River, though by nature murky and silty, nonetheless made for an adequate, if unappetizing, drinking source. But in recent years a man-made problem, giardia, has made drinking untreated river water foolhardy. Giardia's original vector was domestic cattle, but it has now passed from livestock to become endemic among the abundant beaver population of the Qu'Appelle. The water-borne bacterium is not fatal to humans, but it can cause intestinal cramps severe enough to raise doubts in those afflicted.

To solve the problem I had invested in a Swiss army water filter. Switzerland is too clean and prosperous to be an interesting nation, but it does excel at making small things well: pocket knives, watches, optics, pharmaceuticals—and filters. Along the banks of the muddy river it often took a few minutes to find a firm stone base on which to brace the filter. I had to search carefully, too, for a secure foothold before pumping. It was hard work, like inflating a bike tire to high pressure with a cheap hand pump, but I was grateful for Swiss ingenuity all the same. For his part Serge could drink straight from the river without consequences. I envied him his iron stomach, but not his style; his slurping was audible at thirty metres.

On this hot afternoon, my pumping work complete, I slid into the river, grateful for its opaque flowing coolness. Serge remained highly suspicious of both me and full-body immersion and kept his distance accordingly. He was content to splash to dog's knee depth in the shallows. For over an hour we rested in and along the river. The water was refreshing, a rejuvenating indulgence, and my submerged body was blissfully safe from mosquitoes, very few of which ventured out over the middle of the river. My brain cooled to a dreamlike state, drained of higher thought. It was a primal organ, my rumbling stomach, that insisted we leave the river.

Serge's single daily meal was a modest 300 grams of high protein dog food. It was enough: he neither gained nor lost weight and his coat held a healthy sheen. Most pet dogs, like most of their owners, are overfed. Like Serge's, my meal was also dehydrated, and although the packaging was slick, I suspected its constituents and taste were similar to Serge's rations. But I had worked up such a hunger that this thought did not trouble me. I fired up my little portable camp stove and waited impatiently for packaged protein to simmer into a gelatinous but edible mass. After the meal I enjoyed a mug of strong black tea. It was a practical routine: one hot meal per day after settling on an overnight campsite. The rest of the time I got by on a steady high-energy feed of nuts, raisins, chocolate, and dried fruit.

Although I was concerned both about the next day's route and about future problems with heat, fatigue won me a heavy sleep. I rose in darkness to strike camp, and we set off in predawn dimness. The route was initially easy along an old homestead trail, but eventually the trail dwindled to wheel tracks leading through alfalfa hay flats. The last tire impressions petered out at the edge of a marshy wasteland. Progress was still possible, but it was a slow, wet slog. We were crossing a series of natural springs that trickled out of the bottom of the valley walls. Such springs, fed by rain and snowmelt on the flatlands above, are a common feature in parts of the valley; the valley lakes themselves are largely fed by spring water. Outcrops of bush and thicket emerged from the soggy soil, sometimes seizing the travois in their tangles. When this happened Serge would stop and wait patiently for me to return to work the travois free.

Several times I considered trying to get above the problem by climbing the valley walls, but the springs had fostered the growth of an impenetrable barrier of bush across the slopes. There was no alternative but to carry on through the wetlands below. It was several mucky hours before we finally broke through onto dry earth again, as grateful as mariners making landfall after a long sea voyage.

We rested as I cleaned my boots and feet in a final spring that flowed cleanly down a narrow stony defile. The river here ran close up against the hillslopes, and there were a few half-abandoned farm buildings, looking more industrial than most. This place had once had a name, Hyde, and had served as a pumping station supplying water to the railway running above and north of the valley. It was a peaceful setting in which to regather strength before moving on down-valley in an emergency pair of dry boots.

Shortly after noon we stopped for the day in a farmer's hay flat. It was hot again and I was exhausted; for some time I had been carrying all of Serge's baggage. There was a spring for drinking water alongside the hay flat and some bordering brush provided much-needed shade. Determined to join more sensible mammals in their somnolent approach to the midday sun, I managed to pitch the tent and then crawled in to devote myself to sleep and little else for the rest of the day and the ensuing night as well.

Next morning dawned calm, with the promise of further heat. Red-tailed and Swainson's hawks were soon soaring in the thermals rising from the valley walls. Ahead of us the air shimmered over the trail. In this July sun the travois appeared almost useless, and Serge seemed more a burden than of practical use. The walking was easy, but again I had to shoulder Serge's pack. The prospect of a perpetual trade-off of worry, either about Serge if he pulled travois weight, or about myself if I shouldered our combined gear in the heat and mosquitoes, was discouraging. When we reached that day's destination, the provincial park at Crooked Lake, we found that the forecast was for increasingly hot weather. Yet after five days of travel we had not yet reached the geographic midpoint of our journey. I considered carefully—ambition, common sense, and pride all warring within me. Common sense won: for the time being, we would go no farther.

Oblivious to the emotions churning inside me, Serge sat motionless at the park beach, staring at a retriever. The unknown dog was joyously charging far out into the lake in pursuit of his master's sticks. Serge's eyes were narrowed and his hydrophobic expression made plain that for him this was an astonishing sight.

The humour of the situation helped me to control my disappointment. I could not resist the tease. Very deliberately I picked up a stick, threw it into the lake, and looked at Serge expectantly. He studiously pretended not to notice.

My sister collected us from Crooked Lake. Of a practical mind, she brought me clean socks. Margaret is the kind of sister from whom kindness drops unthinkingly, scattered as freely as the down of the Plains cottonwoods in June. Placed against her natural goodness, your own faults seem jagged and magnified. She is a middle child and content to be so.

The drive back to Katepwa was partly in the valley. It was a disturbing experience to pass through valley landscape so effortlessly on sprung steel, shielded by air-conditioning from the outside realities of heat and mosquitoes, watching once striven-for landmarks on the far side of the valley glide by without meaning. In my depressed state of mind the ease of this return journey was in danger of making the struggles of our outbound effort seem laughable and the journey's romance naive. Having returned Serge and me to our starting-point cottage on Katepwa Lake, my sister kindly left me. I settled into a long solitary reflection.

The inventors of the travois, the Dog Age peoples, wintered in small, scattered, family-based groups in valleys, coulees, or wooded hills. In such sites there was adequate shelter, wood, and water to pass the cold season, and by wintering in dispersed groups people could avoid placing too much strain on the game and fuel resources of a small area. In the spring, people migrated out of their wintering camps to meet with relatives and friends for socializing and for the communal buffalo drives on the open Plains. In the autumn, the procedure reversed and the tribal nation broke up again into smaller units. Dogs, I reasoned, would have been most useful in the two migration seasons moving to, from, and along places like the Qu'Appelle Valley. This might have been especially true of the fall migrations when, with luck, the dogs would have been fully employed dragging a heavy supply of dried buffalo meat to winter quarters. Of course, dogs would have been employed year-round in moving local game kills or firewood, but the fall migration must have been when they truly earned their keep. Certainly I had demonstrated that a dog was of very limited utility in the full heat of summer. I determined to be patient, to keep both Serge and myself in good condition, and then to try to continue in September from where we had left off in July.

True to this plan, every summer's day we wandered together on the valley slopes and deep into coulees, normally in the mornings, sometimes again in the evenings. Serge was by now expert with travois and rarely got caught out by bush or slope. In a few isolated tracts along the valley edge there were remnants of native prairie, virgin, unbroken, too awkwardly placed for the plough and too small to be worth fencing for cattle. On these precious headlands of rich, resilient prairie wool the travois was silent, frictionless, almost magical in its passage, flowing over the prairie with no more effort than the hawks above drifting in the thermals. Sometimes I stooped to admire the tangled grasses. The thick blade litter underfoot shielded the hidden soil from wind and sun, insulated it from extremes of heat and cold, held fast the precious spring snowmelt, and filtered the pounding thunder-rains of summer gently down to earth and root. The end result was a marvelous self-generated microclimate a few inches thick. The travois was so perfectly suited to this ancient Plains environment that I was drawn to stop in wonderment and lift the dragging shaft ends to marvel at the burnished gloss of the contact surface, polished to a tawny glow by the prairie grasses, as lovely as diamond willow turned in the hands of a craftsman. At such moments a dim understanding of the purity and grace of old travois travel would stir inside me as I struggled to imagine a sea of the old grasses stretching out beyond valley's edge, as infinite as the toplands around me.

At other times my attention was drawn away from Plains-scale meditations to the fascination of the world of the dog. Serge's sense of smell led to new insights when I tried to decipher what particular animal trail he was following from other clues: tracks, droppings, broken or bent grass. Once I matched Serge nostril for nostril, identified the quarry by smell alone, and understandably lost all interest in further investigation. But Serge diligently pursued to the end and led us to scattered shreds of skunk fur picked clean of flesh. Coyote prints, embedded deep in wet earth, gave the story away. Yet as grateful as I was to Serge's keen senses for their ability to lead me to unsuspected natural treasures, Serge was not always a boon companion, for at times his noise and motion would put wildlife to flight or into hiding.

Only once in this summer interlude did we experience serious excitement. Every night I left Serge tied by a lead to a white spruce in the cottage yard. I slept in a tent not far off. Early one morning, stretching up into consciousness from a deep sleep, I noticed a formless mass on the edge of Serge's lead range. Serge lay belly to the ground, opposite and as far removed from the unknown object as the lead allowed. His eyes stared intently into the distance, acknowledging neither my gaze nor the presence of a foreign body. Puzzled, I stepped closer.

My nose solved the mystery first; it only remained for the eyes to survey the details of the death and disembowelment of *Mephitis mephitis*. Turning from the gutted corpse, I moved towards Serge, keeping just out of contact range, and found to my great surprise and relief that he smelled only of dog. I studied him with heightened respect, leavened with apprehension. Serge wagged his tail hopefully, but I remained suspicious, still avoiding contact. Rabies was endemic in the valley and skunks were the major carriers. There were two reasonable scenarios that would account for a skunk moving into range of a staked-out dog. The first was deliberate rabies-fired aggression. The second was unintentional contact resulting from the carelessness of an overconfident scavenger, probably a juvenile. This latter possibility seemed the more likely, for the neat incision at the scruff of the skunk's neck suggested that Serge had taken the intruder unawares and killed it instantly. But I could not be certain and, as rabies can take up to six months to develop, it was best to get the corpse tested.

It was a Saturday morning, with a hot weekend forecast, and the government laboratory for disease testing would not reopen before Monday. I donned rubber gloves, picked up the corpse, triple bagged it, and then stuffed it into the refrigerator's freezer compartment. This proved to be an error. The bags were guaranteed as airtight, yet even the three of them together could not prevent the reek of fresh-frozen skunk from permeating the refrigerator. The smell was a remarkably effective appetite inhibitor and I consequently ate little that weekend. Monday came, finally, and I delivered the cadaver for testing. A few days later I received news that the skunk had tested negative for rabies, for which I was properly thankful, yet I could have done without the lingering malodor in the refrigerator, a most unaesthetic *memento mori*. In sum, the incident left me with further admiration for wolf-dog Serge, an offbeat dietary marketing opportunity (*eau de mouffette*), and a refrigerator for sale at a very fair price.

By mid-September temperatures had cooled enough to make the journey's restart possible. I drove back to Crooked Lake with Serge and travois, my thoughts racing faster than the car wheels, hope and doubt warring in my brain. On the one hand, I was convinced I was both more experienced and better prepared than in July, and we had the cooling weather in our favor. On the other hand, there was a stream of possible failure scenarios generously supplied me by my overactive imagination. It was a relief to arrive at Crooked Lake where I could set mind and body to work at practical tasks. After pitching tent for the night, I readied the travois in preparation for an early morning start. I loaded it with a kilogram or two more than in summer; Serge would easily be able to handle a little more weight given the lower fall temperatures. Despite my hopes for a September killing frost, the mosquitoes, while not nearly so numerous as at their murderous July peak, still attacked voraciously as twilight dimmed. But dawn, cold and gloomy-grey, brought a different challenge. Mosquitoes were driven to ground by the strong headwind that pushed westward up the valley, driving a hard rain into our faces as we set off eastward. As the hidden sun rose, the temperature fell to just above freezing, the wet felt wetter, the cold felt colder, and my stamina slipped away as I plodded forward, head deeply bowed to the rain gods. In this stretch of the valley there was nowhere to shelter from the elements. We stayed on the move while I processed instant energy from frequent mouthfuls of trail mix.

While I struggled, Serge thrived. Now it was his body, low and streamlined to wind and rain, that held the advantage. He pulled his load enthusiastically and had extra energy to spare for exploratory ventures off to the flanks. He even made the occasional foray ahead of me. While Serge could gaze into the wind with hardly a blink, to see ahead at all I had to squint until my forehead ached. During the last ice age in central Asia the epicanthic fold evolved to reduce the solar glare reflected from snow and ice into the eyes of the Mongoloid peoples. Does the fold help, too, to protect against the gusts of the open Steppes? I lacked any advantage that recent genetic adaptation might convey. Certainly the rounded human eye, to my windblown prairie mind, is poorly adapted to the grasslands challenge of peering into strong winds.

By midafternoon there were two unlikely arrivals at Round Lake: one fresh and cheerful husky, one tired and deep-chilled human. Here, in a casual articulation of beauty, the Qu'Appelle River broadens and deepens into a valley-spanning waterway. It is a quiet recreational oasis for the prairie folk living on the flatlands north and south. It was my good fortune to find the lake not quite deserted; a small cafe was open near water's edge. It was bliss to escape the wind and rain, and luxury to taste the bite of strong coffee. Outside, the temperature continued to fall until, as the sky darkened, the rain turned to heavy snow. Compared to rain at freezing point, snow is the traveller's friend. This night's fall was clean and neat, thick and warm. I slept content.

The next morning dawned as cool and timeless as jade. We arose to a perfect blanket of cleanest white; husky weather had arrived. The sky was calm and clear. From the east brightening blues crept silently up the heavens into infinity, as pure as the first day of creation. Then the sun god himself edged over the black horizon line and flared blinding light into the fresh-born landscape; sky and snow coalesced in a shimmering union of pearly luminance. The lightest of winds bent the tall grass heads that poked through the snow, adding shadow play to this new world of white. The valley lay open and inviting ahead, and I trod with an easy step through cooled midgrass country. Like a well-made sled, the travois slid almost silently over the snow with just the faintest hiss from the dragging shaft ends. As the sun rose, in stillness the snow melted under us, soaking into the soil, unlocking the warm, rich scent of the good earth beneath us. If the fragrance was strong enough to tickle my feeble sense of smell, how intoxicating it must have been for Serge; for him this rush of earthen sensuality must have been druglike in its power!

At the eastern end of Round Lake we travelled straight through a small summer camp, idyllic in its setting, neat little white buildings gleaming in a field of Kentucky bluegrass beaded with snowmelt. Church camps are common around the valley lakes. Out of season they are normally deeply lonely places, for every empty building and every worn pathway—to dining hall, to beach, to chapel, to the assembly bell on a hill—speaks of communal living. In season, the intensity of youthful life—"Hurry, you'll miss it!"—is amplified by the urgency of the fleeting prairie summer. The cabin walls are covered by the graffiti of young souls seeking support and stability in unfamiliar surroundings; "forever friends" is a typical invocation scratched into wood or paint in this most fleetingly temporal of institutions. There are also the predictable scrawls of slightly older campers fired by hormones and the summer sun.

If disquietingly ephemeral in occupancy, these camps are comfortingly timeless in their basic hedonistic premise. Weeks earlier, on a visit to a camp in the valley where I had worked years before, I had found the outdoor emphasis unchanged; computers had been added to impress gullible parents, but were fortunately abandoned in practice. The confusing but common convention of running on "camp time," where camp watches are set one hour behind local time, was still maintained. The clock shift is an example of one of many little stratagems employed to screen off the outside world and intensify the isolated communality of camp life. Visitors to a camp in session, outsiders to an inward-focused community, are politely shunned by most camp employees. But there will always be one or two staff suffering under the pressure of enforced conviviality and conformity who will look upon the autonomy of the visitor with envy. The camper, too, who does not fit in finds camp a painful experience. For the natural loner there is no escape from relentlessly communal eating, sleeping, and sport.

I did find a few physical changes to the old camp. Two familiar buildings had vanished and a huge new multipurpose hall, built of cedar in West-Coast-kit style, dominated the scene. In design, materials, and scale, it was an outstanding example of insensitivity to site. By contrast, a new climbing wall integrated into the old dining hall was a clever innovation in keeping with the outdoors spirit of camp. There had been a political shift as well. Camp councilors now went by environmentally correct names like Mouse, Rock, and Burdock, and there was a discussion, the logic of which I could not follow, as to whether the old Indian cabin names like Cheyenne, Pawnee, and Cree were still socially acceptable. The camp's mission directive emphasized cooperative games.

Yet sun, sand, water, and outdoor pursuits still dominated the day; campfires, nonsense sing-alongs, and quite terrifying ghost stories still filled the night. Most people, whether campers or councilors, seemed happy and tired. The campers were exhausted by the vigorous outdoor schedule; the councilors by the campers. Already bone-weary at day's end, councilors, aged mostly in their late teens or very early twenties, were kept awake late into the night by the fear of missing out on some undefined happening. Little is known of this indeterminate and unspoken event, except that it is certain to occur if you are not there, and if missed will result in a lifetime of regret. As everyone stays up, the event never occurs, but fully half the staff are consequently ill with exhaustion throughout the summer in this otherwise healthiest of locales and lifestyles.

During my visit I tested the food, and found it good—the most important person in any camp is not the director but the cook. It was a camp cook (whose surname was, in fact, Cook) who once explained to me the mystery of the galley hands toiling to reduce potatoes and meat to bite-size chunks: campers, and people in general, eat less when presented with their food in small bits. The current camp staff humoured me, the old employee, by discussing camp history, which naturally sorts itself into the summer regimes, single or multiple, of succeeding camp directors, just as monarchs define English history. I myself had served under the firm hand of John the First, still a known and respected name to the current camp councilors. I recalled to them the earlier extended reign of King Muggsy, a formidable figure, renowned in his time not for his undoubted organizational talents but rather for his camp-astounding ability to walk fifty metres on his hands. This feat, and Muggsy himself, once considered worthy of undying fame, were now unknown to the current staff even as legend.

Of all camp rituals from my own staff days, flagbreak remains rooted deepest in my mind. Every morning campers and staff gathered round a glinting steel pole, product of a far-off foundry, to show their respect to the nation's flag. It was an imported militaristic ritual, quite unfamiliar to the undisciplined, egalitarian children of the Plains. As staff, we took turns offering a few words of dawn wisdom. Since no one was clear what flagbreak was really for, you were free to say what you liked.

Feeling mischievous, when it was my morning to speak I asserted that the flag's familiar stylized maple leaf was a foreign symbol from a foreign tree, imposed on the grassland West by an eastern land of trees and factories. As I spoke, my words were lifted, chopped, and scattered with the prairie dust by gusts of wind pushing through our strange assembly and carrying my thoughts God knows where. A circle of puzzled eyes squinted back at me in the bright prairie sun. I looked up and away to see the wind rippling the grass on the hillslopes into shimmering sun-bronzed waves that flowed down to the lake, bending and sighing to the waters below. For a moment the valley felt timeless, composed of nothing but the purest of prairie elements: space, wind, sun, and precious water. In such a context my unexpected appeal to western regionalism seemed laughably small-minded. Just what was my point? It was too early in the morning for a coherent sense of grievance and, if aggrieved, to what end? Did I intend to propose needle-and-thread grass for a new regional flag? Was I preaching revolution and a new grassland constitution? Everyone stood motionless, until with relief I heard the call for the single-file march to the dining hall. Inside awaited us the down-to-earth realism of the communal daily breakfast of cold cereal and toast, milled from the wheat of the honest prairie soil below us.

It was with such camp memories crowding my mind that I surveyed the neat little site at Round Lake. I was pleased that, though empty, this camp was so small and pristine that out-of-season melancholy could find no hold. I felt in perfect scale with the little cabins, and it was impossible not to feel optimistic. The weather was perfect, and ahead lay the river valley and open country free of serious obstacles. There was only walking, and walking, and walking—kilometre after kilometre of motion, in the way and at the speed the human mind and body were created for.

After seven hours of near-continuous progress in a cool and peaceful valley, I pitched tent in a sheltered hollow near the river. We had covered about twenty-seven kilometres without incident. I was inclined to agree with anthropologist Hubert Smith's judgment for the eighteenth century prairies that "a good rate of travel for a party on foot would have been about 18 miles a day." Today had been not only our lengthiest day of travel but also by far the most enjoyable. The snow had destroyed the mosquitoes, and in the crisp autumn coolness it was quiet joy to be alive.

Over the next two days we made steady and uneventful progress, enjoying September sunshine, light winds, and mild temperatures. On the second day, with tired legs and a tranquil mind, I pitched tent for the night at a forgotten valley historic site, Hamona. In 1895 a community of social idealists with ambitions of allying social and technological advancement founded Hamona along the north valley slopes. The colony was an ideological offshoot of the experimental egalitarian communities of late-nineteenth-century Britain. In theory, if not in practice, the Hamona colonists eschewed the use of money; instead, each member contributed his or her skills to the common wealth in a communal drive for self-sufficiency. The requisite underlying idealism endured for only a few years; internal differences and the lack of a railway link led to the dissolution of the enterprise in 1900. But the colony did not die without issue. The cooperative ethic has taken deep root in prairie soils, and some of the important people in the formation of the now archetypal prairie cooperatives were Hamona alumni.

The site is marked only by a few signboards. Elitist social experiments contemporaneous with Hamona, such as Cannington Manor not far to the south, a failed attempt to re-create the social hierarchy and the squirearchical lifestyle of late-Victorian Britain, do not sit well with prairie egalitarianism. By contrast, the signboard descriptions of Hamona are wholeheartedly admiring and partisan. It is a very modern interpretation, for socialist or cooperative ideals were viewed with suspicion in Hamona's heyday. Most people who emigrated to the prairies fully intended to succeed alone—they sought their family's freedom on a quarter section of freehold. It was the harsh exigencies of life on the northern Plains that forced people into agrarian cooperatism; the burden of the land proved too great for the individual alone. Today both the co-ops and the memories of barn-building bees that issued from collective struggle are sacred on the prairies, but as farm wealth has increased and general circumstances have improved, the immigrants' descendants have preferred individual ownership and control, so far as their finances have allowed. Sharing equipment, even if efficient, is not preferred practice, and true communalists, such as the Hutterites, who pool all property and assets into common ownership, are viewed with suspicion, the more so if they are successful.

In this sense prairie dwellers are fully in the mainstream of Western industrial societies, where individualism is pursued to an extent that baffles and dismays non-Western peoples. Our trademark individualism is a recent development. Craftsmen in medieval Europe, members of a society they perceived as eternal and unchanging, left their works unsigned. The building of the great cathedrals was passed on from generation to generation, and the artisans, building for the public good and the glory of God, died content in anonymity. It would have seemed a sickness to need to single your work out for special notice. It is the great irony of the prairies that individualism here met its match, that those who came in search of social freedom and their own land were quickly driven into some new social contract by a harsh climate and an unyielding landscape. Yet, in forcing us to help one another in spite of ourselves, has this cold prairie land not been kind?

At Hamona only a few old foundations are still visible, with bush and bur oak pushing out of the cavities. The site is overgrown and returning to nature. The European equivalent of old Indian tepee rings, it is a good place for reflection. Here in the valley, broad and solemn, I was at ease with myself, dog, and travois. Travelling partly in another time, I was beginning to shed the constraining shells of identity. My profession, my past, even my name itself, were of no consequence; in the way of the grasslands Indians of old, I was moving closer to living in the here and now. Alonso de Ovalle, an admiring Jesuit, familiar with Pampas Indian life from his grassland traverses of the first half of the seventeenth century, put himself in the mind of the Pampas Querandí and described their perspective in the first person: "Absolute freedom is the greatest good of all. I live here today and tomorrow elsewhere . . . I move here to hunt and there to fish; here to pick the wild fruit and then I move with the season to new harvests; I roam as I will, leaving nothing behind to call or torment me; tragedy cannot reach me for I have nothing to lose; everything is with me, my wife and children follow me, and I have no other needs." In the darkening sky I watched rain clouds gathering. My mind, tiring, turned on thoughts of an earlier age, until dusk and water fell together from the sky. I lay sheltered inside my tent as the rain dropped heavily on tight-woven nylon, softening tomorrow's trail.

For the next day and a half we worked our way down-valley with reasonable ease. But at its eastern end the valley widens and flattens. On the shallow slopes the bush and trees crowd ever closer. Hillside springs become frequent, and with them marshy gullies and barriers of tangled brush. Threading a trail through these slope lands became almost impossible. The route out of the valley, to the toplands, was blocked by vegetation. The other possible way forward, via the valley bottomlands, remained open, but here the ground underfoot became increasingly marshy. Unsure of how to proceed, I found and spoke at length with the last Saskatchewan rancher in the eastern valley. His directions were complex, but they confirmed that it was possible, in theory at least, to get through to a trail on the Manitoba side of the provincial boundary.

On his advice Serge and I initially tried to pick a slope route through the bush, but we were soon hopelessly blocked and driven down to the bottomlands. Progress there was messy but possible for a few kilometres, until a broad marsh blocked the route. A mucky cattle trail leading back into the north-slope bush was then the only option. The wet gumbo sucked at my leather hiking boots, and then oozed over the uppers and down to my toes. Under these challenging conditions Serge yet again proved his good sense. Keeping his distance, he carefully watched my progress ahead. If he thought it sensible, he followed on, but if I got stuck or had other difficulties, he searched out an alternative route through gluelike mud and knotted bush. Miraculously, he only twice became trapped with the travois. Each time he waited patiently for my return and liberating hands.

How to understand the patience and faith that Serge seemed to give without question? There was no doubt that our bond of mutual trust had been strengthened by the passage of so much time alone together. I could have lost his faith through evil treatment, but the core of it had been there, unearned, from the beginning. What was its origin? I had long since ceased to think of Serge as some kind of assistant or junior; he was a full and equal partner. But it remained up to me to pick a route and to decide what should and what should not be undertaken. Sometimes the innocence of Serge's loyalty lay like a burden, a troublesome gnawing at my sense of responsibility. Many, including as eminent and professional a student of animal behavior as Lorenz, have called the close relationship that can develop between a human and a dog "love." Fairly so, for we have all seen that for some people the measure of the death of a favourite dog can be deep and lasting sorrow, and for dogs, too, the death of a benevolent "master" can be unbearable.

Somewhere in the hillslope bush we crossed the Saskatchewan-Manitoba boundary and somewhere in the midst of that tangled brush I pitched tent for the last time. High above us on the flatlands beyond valley's edge I could hear the trains passing on the Canadian National mainline. I moved carefully, trying to take advantage of the few spots of dry ground around the tent. Surrounded by undergrowth as we were, there was nowhere to go and not much to look at. I was anyway tired from the long struggle through bush and mud, so I was content to crawl into the tent at the first signs of dusk. In the darkest of nights and from the deepest of sleeps I was startled awake by the threatening snarl of a wolf outside the tent door—but no, it was only Serge dealing with a real or imagined intruder. "I hope it's not a bear," I thought drowsily, then, "Deal with it, Serge!" I advised confidently. The snarling toned down to a growl and I drifted back to sleep. Serge was, after all, the wonder wolf-dog who had dealt so efficiently with a previous uninvited nocturnal visitor, successfully emerging with his canine body odors inviolate.

We pushed on early next morning. It was slow going and scrappy work, but by early afternoon we finally emerged from the bush onto a dirt road that led eastward to the village of St. Lazare. The river ran slow and silent nearby. The confluence of the Qu'Appelle and Assiniboine Rivers was now only six easy kilometres away. The final steps would be almost a formality, but now that success was assured I felt in no hurry to close the journey. Instead, Serge and I took shelter from the cool wind in a grassy south-facing hollow set deep into the riverbank. I picked idly with my jack-knife at the strata of mud caked on my boots. Slowly, cured brown leather re-emerged, followed by the stiff black rubber of boot sole. The Qu'Appelle's lazy meanders seemed to suggest that its muddy waters, too, were in no hurry to push on to St. Lazare and the Assiniboine or beyond to their ultimate destiny, the icy shallows of Hudson Bay. The bank hollow cupped the weak September sunshine and encouraged us to follow the river's sensible example and snooze at peace in the sun.

Outside St. Lazare I unhitched Serge's travois and stashed it and much of our camping gear in the bush. This would save me having to explain ourselves to the good citizens of the village. We were a rough-looking pair on arrival, a muddy unkempt stranger with a silent husky close to heel. As time passed while we waited for a lift, I was disappointed by my banal hunger for fast-fry foods. That I felt no great elation at journey's end did not disappoint me, but a yearning for hot pig fat was a sad coda to adventure. Surely, I thought, trying to distance my introspection from my stomach, I should be able to extract a higher meaning out of the journey than a gut preference for grease.

Modernity arrived at dusk in the machined angles of a friend's black and silver Nissan truck. We collected the hidden travois and gear. This time the shock of too-fast travel back to Katepwa was eased by the blackness of night.

AT KATEPWA Serge was with me for only a few days more before I had to return him to Jim and Elaine and to sled training for the coming racing season. On a cool and sunny day in late September we wandered together up the slopes to the top of the valley for the last time. From the edge of the infinite flatlands I looked down on the provincial park at Katepwa Point, the government lawns still a deep, dark, chemical green, their irrigated otherness admired by city and rural dweller alike. The leaves of the trees on the point were still verdant as well, spared the first frosts by the stored summer heat of the surrounding waters. A few days a year, like its sprawling asphalt cousins at Echo Provincial Park not far up-valley, the Katepwa Point parking lot is full to overflowing with visitors' vehicles. But today, more typically, it shone black and empty in the sun, witness to a mixture of prairie optimism and waste.

Above the emerald point the valley slopes wore their tastefully muted autumn hues; on the prairies there is little of the intemperate color extravagance of the eastern forests in fall. Among the dominant rusty browns and pale yellows of the hill folds, a few ash trees stood out lemon-bright. Chokecherry bushes wore reddish leaves, echoed on the grassy hill spurs by the ruddy purple tussocks of little bluestem after frost. A light breeze swayed the grass and tugged at leaves; the air was almost painfully crisp and dry. Turning, I wandered east along the valley edge with Serge following. The grass was packed where deer had bedded down between fallow land on our left and the bush reaching up to valley's edge on our right. Harris's and tree sparrows, disturbed in their autumn seed hunt, shot up into the bushes from the ground ahead of us. Propped on a wobbling branch, a chipmunk spun chokecherries expertly in tiny paws, devouring the flesh and then dropping the seed. Every living thing was fattening up in advance of the great prairie winter to come or, like the bush and trees on the slopes below, shutting down until spring. Even the grasses underfoot were in retreat, pulling nutrients from their withering blades down underground and safe into their roots. On the spare branches of the aspen the leaves were thinner now, and I listened to their whispered farewell song:

> I do not know a place so lonely as on prairie's edge,
> with poplar leaves akimbo in the wind;
> that sound so sweet, near ecstasy,
> is loneliness distilled.
>
> The leaves lean back at zephyr's lightest touch,
> yet tightly hold to twig and bough,
> till drained of blood, by autumn gale,
> fly out to bent and withered grass;
> which, thankful for a summer's music,
> welcomes them to soil.

Melancholic, I turned and headed back down the hills to take Serge north, home, away from my beloved prairies to the dark forest lands and the snows he loved.

CHAPTER FOUR

CANOE

OF THE EXTRAORDINARY RIVER
VOYAGES OF PRAIRIE NAVIGATORS

THE IDEA of a voyage down the Qu'Appelle River evolved, I believe, from my own independent ruminations, from the comfortable, indulgent speculations of a well-fed Plainsman on the cusp of the twenty-first century. But who can say where an idea begins? I may well owe the germ of my plan to the inspiration of others. What is certain is that no sooner was I aware of my fluvial ambitions than my imagination was fired by the obsession of a stranger, a man from another time and a far-away country. A farmer, a builder, a brutally strong giant, a desperately homesick Finn trapped in the arid prairie ocean in the years between the great wars—it was difficult to imagine anyone more unlike myself.

Yet here I stood on the physical expression of that stranger's dreams, a fantastical vessel of wood and iron. I swayed high above the prairies, legs braced amidship, leaning into the wind, scanning all horizons. Underneath me the good ship, the mad ship, the *Dontianen*, creaked and groaned with the wind, stranded like its maker countless miles from the Arctic waters it was built for, but will never see. Not far away runs a nameless tributary to the Moose Jaw River, which itself flows north to the Qu'Appelle; here on the *Dontianen* I was only a few kilometres from the ill-defined divide between the Qu'Appelle and the Old Wives Lake watersheds. Water a kilometre or two to the southwest never reaches any sea; it languishes in a basin with no outfall until sucked up by hot sun and thirsty prairie wind. Such a basin is a metaphor for Tom Sukanen's life.

Sukanen came to the prairies like thousands of others, ambitious or desperate or foolhardy, eager to own land and driven by the hope for prosperity that was denied him in his homeland. Like most dry-land settlers he failed to root himself in this strange and naked new land. It was commonplace for prairie immigrants to yearn to return to their homelands and routine for them to fail as farmers. The archaeology of prairie failure—abandoned homesteads, houses, schools, and churches—had become familiar to me on my walk down the valley. But of all who yearned to leave, only one built an ocean-going ship in the midst of the prairie dust.

It was, from the start, a hopeless undertaking. Sukanen's planned river route to Hudson Bay and a sea voyage home unavoidably included innumerable shallows and rapids—difficult with a canoe, inconceivable with an ocean vessel. Yet Sukanen, like many prairie settlers, by nature or by circumstance self-reliant, was remarkably inventive. A sewing machine, a violin, a chronometer, a machine for puffing wheat, a periscope which he used to survey the prairies like a U-boat captain surfacing at sea, all were products of his isolated ingenuity. As the dust bowl thirties dried out land, lakes, and the hearts of men around him, Sukanen turned his genius to shipbuilding. Carefully he accumulated sea charts for the long Arctic voyage home from Hudson Bay to Finland. For six long years he worked on his ship. From raw steel he fashioned rivets, chains, gears, and boilers; from raw wood he constructed a hull, keel, and superstructure. As money and food grew scarce, and as his health declined, Sukanen struggled to complete his strange vessel. He slaughtered and consumed his horses one by one, pulled out his rotting teeth with his ship's pliers, and, ultimately, subsisted on rough-ground wheat which he chewed with his home-forged steel plate dentures. By 1936 he was ready to drag his vessel the twenty-seven kilometres from his homestead to his intended launch site, the South Saskatchewan River. Ahead of his ship he drove an anchor post deep into the earth and with the aid of pulleys, barbed wire cable, and his one remaining horse he winched the vessel forward, inch by inch, until the ship had reached the post. Then he dug up the post, his Plains anchor,

The ship 'Dontianen'

and redrove it into the ground six metres farther ahead and winched again. And so the *Dontianen* crept on over the endless uncaring plain. It was no less than the legend of Sisyphus come alive: Greek turned to Finn, Hell to the Plains.

Sukanen's ship never reached the river. In the end, neighboring farmers and the police collected the would-be mariner from the prairie, malnourished and too weak to lift his hammer, his mind broken and consumed by his nautical mono-mania. On a most curious open-prairie charge of obstruction of His Majesty's Thoroughfare he was packed off to die in an asylum, leaving the *Dontianen* stranded amid grass and sky.

Years later the good people of Moose Jaw recovered Sukanen's ship and docked it where I now stood on the open prairie a few kilometres south of the city, where the ship, prow pointed to Finland, is intended to serve as a "monu-ment to the early pioneers." The effect on the modern prairie traveller would be greater if the vessel were standing in isolation, but directly adjacent lies a mock-up Main Street of a vanished prairie town, shop fronts and boardwalks and the grim rusting tools of the frontier dentist. Nonetheless, the ship still stands as an astonishing singularity: unlike the reconstructed blacksmith's shop nearby, you cannot ignore the *Dontianen*; its existence demands an attempt at human understanding.

For me, the seeds of Sukanen's madness were easy to understand. Homesickness and loneliness I knew; I had experienced the edge of their soul-corroding power myself, as most all of us sometime do. Foreigners on the prairies, isolated by language, culture, climate, and distance, were always in danger of cracking, exploding like the bark from a prairie tree when the desiccating wind sucks out the suppleness and the frost bites too deeply. It was not the fact but rather the expression of Sukanen's madness that fascinated. Many travellers had turned to maritime imagery to describe their journeys over the prairie: the ox-drawn cart was christened a prairie schooner; the rolling hills were said to undulate like ocean waves. Lacking terrestrial landmarks, prairie travellers took bearings at night by the stars and at noon by the sun, as if in mid-ocean. The grass itself was a wind-tossed sea to many chroniclers. But in Sukanen's mind these oceanic metaphors became reality.

I planned to travel in a more modest, though noble, craft, the canoe. It would be a different route than that planned by Sukanen, and my objective was prairie discovery, not prairie escape; I wanted to understand the prairies, not to flee them. But the image of Sukanen's dream-ship has never left me. Often I found myself pondering his vision during the planning and execution of my prairie voyage. His madness is noble to me now. May the prairie wind blow the scent of Finnish pine to his restless spirit.

IT IS NOT Sukanen and the *Dontianen* but rather the fur traders and their canoes which northern prairie children are taught to think of as noble and romantic, as quintessentially Canadian, as icons of the nation's wild country spirit. A former prime minister, Pierre Trudeau, is one of many who have waxed lyrical about spiritual gains won from canoeing in the wilderness. More prosaically, the Canadian federal government supports the prestige of the canoe by dispensing grants to the national Canoe Hall of Fame. In the most recent update of the canoeing parable, Canadian children are taught the Indian origins of the canoe and told of the skills of the First Nations paddlers, as well as of the exploits of the voyageurs, the French-Canadian traders who canoed the continent in search of furs. To suggest that the canoe is ugly, or that the exploits of the voyageurs were trivial or boring, would be a Canadian heresy.

It is not a heresy I would be prone to, for, despite the nation-building agenda that underlies the promotion of a canoe ideology, the respect accorded the craft and its paddlers is well grounded. Explorer Samuel de Champlain was rightfully impressed by the speed, agility, and shallow draft of the Indian canoes that sped to meet him in 1603 when his ship, surveying upstream on the St. Lawrence, reached the mouth of the Saguenay River. The aesthetics of the canoe have always been undeniable. Many are the craftsmen who have admired the sleek lines of a birchbark or cedar-strip canoe and have sought to emulate its beauty. As for historical importance: much of the Canadian-American border was defined by the reach of the canoe (the forty-ninth parallel approximates the boundary between the Mississippi and Hudson Bay watersheds), and the beaver the canoes pursued was the foundation of Canada's economy. Even if you agree with writer Robert Lee that the canoe was "the original instrument of centralist oppression," you cannot sensibly deny its importance.

Yet when I looked back into the navigation history of the Qu'Appelle River, I discovered that the canoe has never been particularly successful on the Canadian prairie. The Plains Indians themselves, though aware of canoes through their woodland neighbors, did not themselves make or use them. The indigenous craft used for river crossings and downstream travel on Plains rivers was the bull boat. Similar in design to the ancient Celtic coracle, the bull boat was a simple, tub-like craft that could be built in a few hours by sewing buffalo skins onto a frame of bent willow branches. As the skins rotted quickly, the boats were not very durable. Nor could they be paddled upstream. Nonetheless, they were useful and well adapted to local resources of skin, willow, and sinew. Anthony Hendry and Matthew Cocking, early explorers on the prairies, both made crossings of the South Saskatchewan River in the 1700s using bull boats, and as late as 1858 surveyor John Fleming could report on the continued utility of the craft: "Hunters and trappers frequently set out from Fort à la Corne, on horseback or on foot to the Moose Woods or the great prairies on the south Saskatchewan, and return in bull-boats laden with dried-meat and skins, both craft and cargo being the proceeds of their hunt."

Of course one-way travel has obvious limitations and bull boats had limited load capacity. By contrast the *canot du nord*, or north canoe, the birch-bark canoe typically employed by voyageurs west of Grand Portage at the head of Lake Superior, could carry a cargo of fourteen hundred kilograms. The north canoe was about eight metres in length, close to a metre and a half in beam, and drew about forty-five centimetres of water when fully loaded. A working crew numbered between five and seven paddlers. The canoe provided good shelter as well as transport; when rain threatened a crew at camp, the canoe was tilted on its edge and a tarp spread from the top gunwale to the ground.

North canoes were magnificent craft and the men who paddled them larger than life. We are fortunate to have excellent written records of their exploits. Although we think of them mainly as adventurers, the fur traders were first and foremost businessmen and the canoe a businessman's tool. Since the ties of commerce stretched from Europe to the heart of North America, excellent recordkeeping was essential business practice. Most written records have survived, thanks in part to the oligopoly or monopoly nature of the fur trade, and the bulk of them are conveniently held together at the Hudson's Bay Company Archives in Winnipeg.

I entered the archives with awe and profound gratitude for their very existence. The archives span the majority of Canadian history and geography. Explorers' reports, expedition diaries, day-to-day fort journals, even the original logs of the ships travelling between Hudson Bay and England from the 1670s on—they are all found here. Records of competing firms, like those of the North West Company and the Hudson's Bay Company, lie united in the files of history. The archive's exterior street face betrays little of its contents or function; it is flat, nondescript, and institutional. It is a peculiarly Canadian celebration of the nation's greatest historical treasure. In countries with more self-awareness such chronicles would be housed under noble domes and framed by soaring columns and arches; there would be spacious reading rooms and dignified furnishings. In reality the impression is that of the basement of a small-town library. Alas, my foolish country!

Many English-speaking Canadians suffer from the damaging misconception that they have no North American history worth thinking about, in contrast to their French-Canadian compatriots, who are thought to suffer from too much, rather like honourary Europeans. The error stems partly from the widespread assumption that the only heritage that matters is written and stored in dusty overseas libraries or visible in European architecture and monuments. Yet people have lived and died and changed the face of the Americas for over ten thousand years. A skilled eye can wander over almost any fallow field on the prairies and pick out the stone tool fragments that bear witness to millennia of occupation. And even those Americans and Canadians who hold to the misconception that history starts only with Europeans live in nation-states older than most in the world. Of history in North America, there is plenty.

If in the archives you despair of a nation's indifference to its past, at least a full-scale replica of the founding ship of the Hudson's Bay Company, the *Nonsuch*, can be found at anchor in appropriate dignity a few blocks away in a Winnipeg museum. From archives to museum it is a fascinating walk through the gritty grid streets of downtown Winnipeg. To make this little journey is to see an entirely different, and very urban, prairie. Winnipeg is the poorest of western cities, inhabited, more than any other Canadian prairie town, by people who "look city," who clearly have been born, live, and will die in the metropolis. The soils here are deep and rich, and the rains dependable, but the memory of the tallgrass prairie that once stretched high to the prairie sun where the city now stands is extinct in the minds of almost all locals, who are also happily oblivious to the great prairie beyond the perimeter highway. In its age, architecture, manufacturing, ethnicity, and pockets of old money, the city, Canada's microequivalent of Chicago, is inward-looking and self-contained.

Every morning I walked the Osborne Street bridge over the Assiniboine River and paused to look down into the silty flow below, as if hoping to separate out the tributary waters of the Qu'Appelle from the greater fluvial whole beneath me. The Assiniboine moved at a measured, dignified pace. The nuances of texture and colour conveyed by its subtle muddy tones, so different to the tumbling crystal flow of a mountain river, hinted at honest, hard-won wisdom, acquired over unhurried kilometres of contemplative travel. I never stopped for long; the roar of rush-hour traffic conspired against reflection and I was anyway always eager to spend a full day in the archives. Time slipped by unnoticed as I delved among the old records, straining to decipher the elegant handwritings of the past. Most journal entries were mundane business notes—the weather always featured prominently, affecting business so directly as it did in those days—but glimpses of personal and landscape experience lay scattered throughout the records. Handwritten as they were, the narratives spoke directly to the reader in the manner of a personal letter, and I caught myself wondering who, if anyone, had read these texts before me. Phrases that would make you groan when reading a B-grade Hollywood script ("I wish there was one man here I could trust.") materialized in the journals as startling historical truth. I marvelled at the stoicism of poor John Sutherland, fur trader, who, upon reaching Brandon House in May of 1794 after nine days paddling down the Assiniboine, wrote, "I have the misfortun to say I shot [off] my Thumb in salooting the place which maks me very mellancholy at presant."

It would have been easy to spend months rummaging in the archives; every journal, log, or report suggested two or three fascinating lines of investigation.

It took discipline to confine myself to the experiences of canoeists on the Assiniboine and its affluent, the Qu'Appelle, and to ignore the fate of traders when they passed out of this area. A year ago at this time I had been outside, rough-hewing wood, stitching skin to travois, picking at slivers and blisters, and inhaling the aromas of living plants and living earth. Now I sat in a climate-controlled, windowless archive, wearing white gloves to protect original documents from natural skin oils, and turning every antique page with care. The contrast in environments could hardly be greater, but the feelings of wonder and anticipation were the same this year as last, and for the same reason: I was soon to be re-creating the original pages of history.

The starting point for my research was the great French explorer La Vérendrye, who was the first to record impressions of canoe travel on prairie rivers. In late September of 1738 he set off on a journey to Mandan territory (in modern-day North Dakota), departing upstream on the Assiniboine from the Forks (modern-day Winnipeg). He was not impressed:

> I found the river very low, no rain having fallen during the summer. Its course is from the west, very winding and very broad, and having a swift current with many shallows . . . I decided to proceed by land following the prairies, with the men I did not need following in canoes, and found the prairie route to be shorter, since it cut across several bends in the stream and one was thus able to keep a straight course. On the evening of October 2, the Indians warned me that I could ascend no farther, the river being too shallow to proceed in canoes . . . Everyone agreed that we could go no farther, and that to do so would be running the risk of rendering the canoes useless upon returning, and in a place lacking materials for refitting. Here there was neither pitch nor roots for that purpose.

Fifty-five years later, in September of 1793, John Sutherland, too, set off up the Assiniboine from the Forks, but his destination was farther upriver, a fort just above the Qu'Appelle River junction. The going was tough, with the party averaging only about nineteen kilometres a day. Tracking and wading were frequently necessary, and Sutherland complained of "the Canoes braking upon old sticks and stumps which is very numeros in this River, and they [the men] having scarcely any pitch or bark to mend them with." John Macdonell kept a journal on the same journey and, like La Vérendrye before him, preferred walking along the valley edge to canoeing the meanders below. On October 5 he noted: "The River continues so crooked all this time that in two hours we can travel as much as the canoes can do from sunrise to sunset." It became a pattern of travel on the Assiniboine for the "gentlemen" to walk or ride across the prairies, hunting for meat for the hard-working canoe crews slogging it out on the twisting river below.

From the 1790s until 1821 the Hudson's Bay Company, the North West Company, and the XY Company all competed vigorously on the lower Qu'Appelle for pemmican supplies. But the Qu'Appelle pemmican trade was fickle; some years would bring a good haul, some years would not. What was constant was the difficulty of maintaining a trading presence on the prairies. Wood was in short supply for fort construction and even for winter fuel. It was often necessary to relocate a fort to new wood supplies every few years. A depressed Hudson's Bay Company trader, John McKay, charged with building a fort on the Qu'Appelle for the winter, wrote in his journal entry for November 18, 1812: "Arrived at River Quappelle . . . and after examining the Country hereabouts . . . finding it very inconvenient for building as it is one of the most destitute places for Wood of any discription I ever saw."

Another problem was unfriendly relations with the Indians. While heading downstream with the spring floods of 1810 on the twisting Qu'Appelle River just east from Round Lake, a trading party led by John MacDonald was ambushed by Indians. Writing at Brandon House in 1815-16, fort master Peter Fidler reported traders being scalped and, more frequently, having horses stolen. The roots of hostilities were to be found in the needs, or greed, of the traders and in the contrasting self-sufficiency of the Plains Indians. As early as 1776 North West Company trader Alexander Henry the Elder lamented: "The wild ox [buffalo] alone supplies them with every thing which they are accustomed to want . . . The amazing numbers of these animals prevent all fear of want; a fear which is incessantly present to the Indians of the north." From the fur traders' point of view, this enviable state of affairs was bad for business. Whisky, therefore, became critical, for the Plains Indians were, as Hudson's Bay Company governor George Simpson wrote in 1822, "so independent of European commodities that they would not take the trouble of hunting in order to provide themselves with any other article." Unfortunately, as the traders themselves were well aware, alcohol was useful only for short-term gain. Over the long term it destroyed Indian health and morale, reduced trade, and led inevitably to mutually suspicious relations and sporadic violence.

Even as he traded them whisky, Daniel Harmon thought the Plains Indians the happiest people on earth, in possession of everything they needed. This was in sharp contrast to his own state, for Harmon seemed to be hungry much of the time. Alexander Henry the Younger agreed with Harmon about the value of independence to the Plains Indians and how alcohol destroyed it. On February 15, 1803, concluding his account of a liquor-induced bout of fighting and killing among Indians near Portage la Prairie, Henry wrote:

The Indians totally neglect their ancient customs; and to what can this degeneracy be ascribed but to their intercourse with us, particularly as they are so unfortunate as to have a continual succession of opposition parties to teach them roguery and destroy both mind and body with that pernicious article, rum? What a different set of people they would be, were there not a drop of liquor in the country! If a murder is committed among the Saulteurs, it is always in a drinking match. We may truly say that liquor is the root of all evil in the North West. Great bawling and lamentation went on, and I was troubled most of the night for liquor to wash away grief.

Yet, however sincerely held, sentiments of admiration for the independent Plains Indian lifestyle and those similar sentiments Father de Ovalle expressed for the Pampas Querandí stopped neither Plains peddler nor Pampas priest from pursuing their respective trades.

The traders had not only the Indians to fear, but also each other—the roguish business competitors that Henry referred to. In 1816, just as Indians had done a few years earlier to them, men of Henry's own North West Company took advantage of the circuitous course of the Qu'Appelle to set up a successful ambush of fur traders, in this case of Hudson's Bay Company rivals. One resulting prisoner, James Sutherland, managed to smuggle a letter out of captivity. It was duly recorded on May 12 by Fidler at Brandon House:

Sir/ on Monday we started from the House [a Hudson's Bay Company fort on the lower Qu'Appelle river], and owing to the shallowness of the river, did not get here [the point of ambush] till yesterday about 8 O'Clock AM, when we were attacked by about 50 Canadians & half Breeds; This is the narrowest part of the River, the Batteaux touch both sides in passing, and is also a shallow rapid and a very crooked reach, which obliged our Boats to be far apart, and out of sight of each other. Two Boats that was a head of mine was disarmed & the men made prisoners, before I knew anything of it; The others behind could render no assistance: when I landed there was upwards of 30 Guns pointed at me . . . I am here with a Guard of Canadians both over my Person & Property and write this in a very hidden manner . . . be on your Guard, as I have no doubt but an attempt will be made on you . . . forward the news to the Governor in chief as fast as possible. I am writing by the light of a very bad fire, therefore must conclude wishing for better times.

Sutherland survived his predicament, and the North West and Hudson's Bay trading companies buried their animosities in the great commercial Union of 1821, ending a romantic era of no-holds-barred frontier competition.

In 1857, when rivalry was only an old memory and a comfortable Hudson's Bay Company straddled the trade alone, Professor Henry Hind was commissioned by the Canadian government to undertake an exploring expedition to study the suitability of the prairie West for settlement and economic development. The professor paid particular attention to the Qu'Appelle, and with grand Victorian enthusiasm envisioned no less than the eventual flooding of the entire valley and its subsequent navigation by great steamships. Hind himself travelled by canoe to assess the navigability of the entire length of the river in its natural state. Indian guides gave him some hint of the climatic variability of the prairie and of the great seasonality in river flow when they told him of flood years when the valley was in places completely submerged from north to south, two and a half kilometres wide, the river in effect becoming a shallow lake. Yet in other springs there would be little snowmelt and a mere droughty scrap of a stream by summer. From Hind's personal experiences it is easy to imagine why he might have begun to brood on permanently flooding what became, for him, a frustrating valley.

In July of 1858 Hind departed westward from Fort Qu'Appelle, heading upstream toward the source of the Qu'Appelle River. A day later, not far upstream from Pasqua Lake, Hind abandoned the canoes to the Métis crew to track upstream, while he himself walked on the toplands above the valley. Like other prairie travellers before him, Hind made better time on foot than the paddlers below, "the windings of the stream involving a course three times as long as a straight line up the valley." After a further three days of travel Hind related how the men he had sent ahead with carts and horses had to await the slower canoes, and how an empty cart was sent back to collect the final laggard. Dispirited by the river, Hind finally gave up on canoe travel entirely:

The tortuous character of the stream before we took the canoe out of the water, may be imagined from the fact that eleven hours constant, steady tracking enabled us to progress only five miles in a straight line through the valley, and not less than 200 courses and distances were recorded in the canoe. Some little time was lost in crossing from one side to the other in order to avoid the willow bushes, which only grew on the inside of a bend, rarely or never on the outside or longest curve . . . The fetid air from the marshes made most of the party feel unwell, and I therefore determined to carry the canoe in a cart on the immediate edge of the prairie, keeping the valley in constant view.

The same day as he himself set off in search of the Qu'Appelle's headwaters, Hind sent his assistant, James Dickinson, on an eastward expedition from Fort Qu'Appelle downstream to the Assiniboine junction. This was the route I intended following, so I keenly hoped for a more positive report than Hind's dismal assessment of the upper half of the Qu'Appelle system. Dickinson at least found paddling "easy work," but complained that the narrow width and "strange contortions" of the river made steering difficult: ". . . the bends of the river are innumerable and very sharp, and the waters sweep round them with great velocity; oftentimes, but for the strong and dextrous arm of the steersman, the canoe would have been dashed against the bank; as it was he could not avoid sometimes getting entangled among the overhanging branches of the willows."

I was suspicious of Dickinson's suggestion that the quiet Qu'Appelle could in places be a raging torrent; perhaps he had embellished his journey's danger to upstage his boss. Yet if Dickinson spoke truly, then I welcomed the challenge of a few rapids. Dickinson also had the usual grumbles about black flies and mosquitoes, but having myself endured the previous summer's extraordinary mosquito outbreak, I felt dismissive about mosquito complaints.

My research led me to conclude that in the hundred or so years of Qu'Appelle fur trade history canoes had been next to useless in all but the lowermost reaches of the river. There, in roughly the final thirty valley kilometres, the water flow was more certain and the hills were more heavily wooded than in the valley farther west. When I considered traders' journals concerning the wider prairies, I saw the same pattern of troubles repeated whenever the river routes led the traders out into true grassland country. A good example was the traders' failure to maintain forts or communications on the South Saskatchewan River. Operating a fragile birch-bark canoe in a land without birch or pitch, both of which were necessary for almost daily repairs, was a next-to-hopeless undertaking. And how were you to build a fort or survive the winter without timber? So, despite the occasional canoe foray into the grassy heart of the prairies, the North Saskatchewan River, which runs roughly along the border of wooded country and the prairie, largely marked the southern boundary of canoe commerce. As the *Dontianen* belongs on the sea, canoes belong on woodland lakes and rivers.

A key contributing factor determining this sad conclusion is the distinction between what the term *watershed* means in the wooded East and what *watershed* implies on the Plains. In the East watersheds are, on the whole, made up of definable rivers and streams flowing reliably to the sea. But on the Plains, a land of flat or undulating topography and barely positive moisture balance, water does not neatly divide up and flow away to the sea down cleanly defined channels. First, of course, internal drainage basins flowing nowhere are common on the Plains. More fundamentally, the primary flows of water on the Plains are vertical, not horizontal. Snowmelt and rain sink down to the water table and percolate back up and down the soil profile with the seasons. The general rule is that the greater the vegetation cover, the greater is the water loss to transpiration. Only occasionally does the soil saturate and do surface waters flow off to some stream or river, and then, as often as not, the flow is a flood event. Alternatively, the water may sink far deeper. Somewhere below a given Plains soil profile may lie an aquifer, a lens of water-bearing sediment; in some places on the Plains they are over four hundred metres thick. In effect, prairie waters can go every which way. On the prairies I have even seen the impossible: the wind moving water—as snow—uphill. Water moving in all directions, and mostly up and down, is bad news for the canoeist looking for a dense network of defined and reliable travel routes.

Very late in the fur trade era there was one final spectacular effort to prove the viability of the river route downstream from Fort Qu'Appelle to the Assiniboine. The Hudson's Bay Company had long since abandoned river traffic in favor of a valley cart trail when, in 1869, on the shores of Echo Lake, an optimistic Archibald McDonald directed the building of a fleet of flat-bottomed boats out of poplar planking. Spruce gum mixed with buffalo grease was used to seal the seams in the absence of proper tar. The boats set off with a full cargo of furs. Fur trader Isaac Cowie described the outcome:

> . . . the batteaux absorbed the water like sponges and leaked like sieves, requiring the crews to be constantly bailing instead of propelling the craft, when it was not compulsory to land the cargo and haul up the boat for repairs. When the "brigade" started the water was at a fairly high stage, and it made fair progress under lodge-leather sails, over the lakes, but the intervening streams were so crooked and offered so many impediments that it was a whole week before they reached the outlet of the second lake [Katepwa] below the fort. "Baffled but not beaten" by all these difficulties, by the daily desertion of the men hired for the trip, by the discontent of the dispirited "regulars," and by the interminable sinuosities of the stream, the determination of Mr. McDonald finally forced the batteaux to Fort Ellice after a period of six weeks' continual driving. Unavoidably, under such circumstances, a great part of the cargo was spoilt; so this experimental voyage ended any further attempts in that direction.

My mind found no peace when I left the archives for the final time, wandered south across the Assiniboine, and stared down into the murky waters. I was excited by the eyewitness accounts of the rivers and prairie of old, troubled by my new understanding that the canoe was, is, and always will be unsuited to the prairies, and firm in my conviction that, with Sukanen's spirit behind me, I was going to canoe the Qu'Appelle anyway.

ABOUT A YEAR after my travels with Serge, my canoe touched Qu'Appelle waters. My craft was a small one, a mere four metres long, and made of fibreglass, a material unknown to the fur traders. I cannot claim my canoe was particularly aesthetic; its chief virtues were its budget price and robustness. I had owned it for years, inherited it in fact from my father—one of the commonest and most satisfying ways to acquire a canoe in Canada. In all my years of ownership I had added only a single element of class to its workaday body: I had replaced the original, rotted, plywood centre thwart with a handmade combination thwart and yoke. This I had created myself by carving, shaping, and sanding a block of Sitka spruce until the yoke surface matched the lie of my shoulder blades and until my fingers had their own personal groove-grips molded into the wood. To accomplish this minor feat of woodcraft had taken me nearly forever, but wherever necessary it allowed me now to make one-man portages with the canoe resting comfortably upside down on my shoulders. The strength of ash makes it the wood of choice for thwarts, but Sitka spruce is much softer and therefore easier to shape. Sitka's long fibers give linear strength, and it is very light, which makes it a good choice for wing ribs in small airplanes as well as for canoe yokes. In truth, the custom gracefulness of my centre thwart only emphasized the mass production look of the body of the canoe. Yet, plebeian duffer's craft that it was, the lines, feel, and handling dynamics of my humble factory model were essentially the same as those of its birch-bark precursors.

I trained for my journey with a simple routine of daily paddling. An early start was always best to avoid the afternoon sun that can be a greater problem on heat-reflective water than on land. I grew familiar with the river downstream from Katepwa Lake, its riffles and small rapids, sandbars and deadheads, overhanging trees and twisting banks. Individually none of the river challenges was very demanding, but there were enough of them, and a strong enough current, that my attention was kept fully engaged. One unwelcome hazard was a barbed wire fence strung across the river. By carefully lifting the bottom strand I could pass beyond, but I wondered how frequent such fences, happily unknown to the fur traders, might be farther downstream. As my later journey would show, it was a naive and happy ignorance.

I varied the river routine with lake paddling, deliberately seeking out wind and whitecaps. Shoulders and arms turned sore, but I found that a few hours' paddling left the body as a whole less tired than walking with a backpack. To build a balanced competence, I made a point of always beginning paddles on my "off," that is, my left, side. For the same reason I varied my seating postures. Draw, pry, and sweep strokes, bracing, paddling backwards, underwater recoveries: I exercised all the fundamentals. Silence on the water was my highest ambition, both for wildlife observation and for its own intrinsic aesthetic. Calm and tranquillity define competent canoe travel; no other man-made motion can equal the magical perfection of silent blade and bow.

Occasionally I caught myself talking to the canoe. I was missing the flesh-and-blood mutual trust that Serge and I had enjoyed. That mammalian bond was, of course, not replaceable by cold fiberglass, but I could seek the sense of balance that is fundamental to successful paddling and strive for almost spiritual oneness with the canoe, where body mass and canoe seem to flow one into another like a strong marriage.

Sometimes, while on a training run, I beached the canoe so as to sit and study the river, its ripples and curls, its colours and reflections. Comprehending the shimmering, ever-changing totality of what I saw was impossible; it was the artist's problem of trying to capture light on canvas or of painting a fire. The best spot of all for river watching was by the plunging waters of the Fort Qu'Appelle weir. At times the water there was astonishingly translucent, revealing minnows in their thousands and larger fish casually finning through the schools. On other days the water was murky or sickly green. Sometimes the surface tension held the scintillating cast-off skins of fish flies, sometimes the soft white seed-down of the nearby cottonwoods. Life of all kinds was drawn to the churn of oxygenated water; iridescent grackles and elegant terns shared the fishing with proud kingfishers and contented men and boys. Swallows appeared and disappeared in webs of interlocking flight.

One very lucky day, just upstream from the weir, I spotted an otter near the bank. A fish had died tangled in a strip of torn netting and the otter was twisting and tearing at the mesh, trying to worry out a full mouthful of flesh. Its body twisted with miraculous flexibility; its hands seemed almost human in their grip- ping technique; sharp white teeth flashed in the sun. What a glorious creation!

It was a short walk from the weir into the centre of town. Prairie towns are a fascinating genre, but most are too much alike to be of interest as individuals. They grew up at the same time, with the same technology, and to the same ends. The structural differences between them are therefore often trivial: one town's roads run north-south and east-west, conforming to the general prairie grid road system, while another's streets are aligned to run parallel and perpendicular to a passing railway; one town's wooden grain elevator (now often abandoned in favour of hideous concrete super-terminals) is near to Main Street, while anoth- er's elevator lies "across the tracks." In their homogeneity prairie towns reflect our future as well as their past, for everywhere in the world cities are advancing to uniformity; the shopping malls, cars, and fast food restaurants of Calgary are now almost indistinguishable from those of Oslo or Auckland. It is a great irony that as destinations everywhere become more accessible they also become more alike, and so less worth travelling to—though in tireless pursuit of novelty we travel all the more.

Fort Qu'Appelle is an exception to prairie homogeneity, owing partly to its beautiful valley floor site, wedged between two lakes, and partly to its curious mix of clienteles. "The Fort," as it is known locally, rests on Echo Creek alluvium. The topography is young; only a few millennia ago moraine rubble, washed out from the southern hills, was fanning out across the valley, splitting Echo and Mission Lakes asunder and building up a rare flat settlement site for a future valley town. Now farmers do their business and take morning coffee at the local service sta- tion. There is a large proportion of farm retirees, as in many other prairie towns, but the Fort is a minor mecca for artists and artisans as well. Summer tourists arrive with the heat and the holidays, and the First Nations communities near the town (some Indian Reserve land is now within the town limits) are growing in political profile and economic importance. The most recent addition to the mélange is the Canadian Navy's summer cadet training school on Echo Lake. Dozens of cadets spill out to populate the Fort's stores and ice cream parlors; dressed in neat black-and-white uniforms, they travel in tight little collectives in a startling penguinesque contrast to the relaxed prairie dress codes of everyone else. The different social groups pursue their affairs in isolation one from another in a style more reminiscent of an East European community prior to the world wars than of a typical prairie town. But the unusual social colour and diversity bring economic stability, a rare achievement on the prairies.

Leaving the Fort, I took mental stock. My paddling skills and fitness were now acceptable, and the observations of those who had travelled before me were deep-set in my mind. My senses were attuned to the river. I was ready for launch.

CHAPTER FIVE

"EN AVANT!"

OF COYOTES, CATTLE, AND WIRE, AND OF THE MANY WONDERS OF THE PRAIRIE RIVER

CANOE AND CANOEIST set off down Katepwa Lake just after sunrise on a morning in mid-July so pure and pristine that I pitied those still pitched horizontal in too-comfortable beds. A night wind had churned any surface algae deep into the lake, but this dawn was calm, with an ethereal mist lifting over cool, clear water. The water was light on the ash paddle blade, no doubt because of the surge of adrenalin that fires the start of any adventure. After an hour's paddle I reached the weir that marked the end of Katepwa Lake and the rebirth of the Qu'Appelle River—my first portage. It was short and easy work.

I was fortunate to find the river still running strongly so long after the snowmelt. There was good depth for my canoe's modest draft. Water quality was good, too, for when the water temperature is not too high and there is a reasonable current the river is well oxygenated. Never on my journey did I find the river green with algae. It was either clear or the muddy brown of a homely prairie stream carrying the silt of the land. Murkiness can be a natural state for many Plains rivers and explains river names like the Red, the (Alberta) Vermilion, or the (Texas) Colorado.

I studied the riverbanks sliding by. The Qu'Appelle was neither a purely erosive high-energy torrent, cutting steeply down into mountain rock, nor a slow and lazy levee or delta-building river, meandering through the flatlands of riverine senility. Instead I was favored with the constant visual interest of both erosion and deposition. The higher, or "cut," bank was typically under active erosion as the water swept round the outside of a bend, while on the opposing, shallower inside riverbank slower-moving water deposited sand and mud. A satisfying intellectual balance, yes, but I could not pretend that the Qu'Appelle was a spectacular or dangerous river in the romantic voyageur tradition, so I took heart in writer Giovanni Guareschi's celebration of the flatland nature of *his* native river. The Po, he said, in 1951, "is the only worthwhile river in Italy: and the rivers one respects develop in the plains, because water is intended to remain horizontal, and only when it is quite horizontal does it possess all its natural dignity. The Niagara Falls are a rather vulgar fair-ground sight, like a man walking on his hands."

Not far downstream from the weir an excited, harsh squawking alerted me to the local hunter. Letting the canoe drift, I peered through my binoculars down the straight reach ahead and spied an angry magpie, some hundred metres distant, low in a bush over river's edge. Magpies are exceedingly intelligent birds. A prairie countryman might well tell you of the sign reading "Don't feed the birds"—and of the magpie casually dropping its wing over the "Don't." This particular magpie had a clear message: "Coyote about; watch out!" The coyote was inspecting the starboard riverbank with feigned disinterest, snuffling here, digging a bit there, then moving on at an unhurried pace. He ignored the magpie above—a sensible strategy, for what else could he do? I remained motionless as the canoe drifted to starboard and gently grounded into the shallows at an angle nearly parallel to the bank, perfect for forward observation. Now the coyote had picked up a scent trail; he abandoned his casual manner and jogged purposefully along the bank toward the canoe, his nose to the ground. With the binoculars pressed tight to my eyes, I was frozen with excitement as the coyote grew in size until he resembled some lost megafauna, so close was his approach. The magpie had fallen silent and there was no breath of wind. *How close could he come?* Finally, not some twenty metres away, the coyote slowed and stopped. He stretched his neck and large ears toward me, lifting and dropping one foreleg uncertainly, his hunter's eyes cooling with doubt, his facial muscles furrowing back tightly. To

River coyote

my magnified vision he appeared a mere body length away. With my motionless shape obscured by canoe and binoculars, it was his twitching nose that finally deciphered the mystery. The shock of canoe-man scent was graphic in the raised neck-hairs, but starker still was the intense fear that pulsed forward from the back of his dilating pupils. He sprang backwards and turned in one fluid motion to flee at full speed down the riverside, then in two leaps cleared the bank and was lost to my sight. I remained lodged in the shallows, shaken by the emotion I had read so clearly in his eyes. Coyotes are regularly shot at on the prairies, so I expected to see fear; it was the clarity and intensity of its expression that unsettled me.

James Dickinson, too, reported a coyote (a "prairie wolf") on his Qu'Appelle canoe journey. Doubtless while rounding a bend, he saw "a little prairie wolf, Togany, as he is called by the Indians, that was standing by the edge of the river, and who was so much astonished at our sudden appearance, that he never thought of running away, but stood staring at us incapable of motion." As I pushed back into the river I was grateful that the cleverness and adaptability of Togany's children had enabled them to thrive on the prairies even today.

The magpie was the first of many birds I saw along the river. It was the fledgling season, and young, foolish birds are often the easiest to spot. Most poignant was the sight of a small, hard-working foster parent, a sparrow, feeding a fat juvenile cowbird shakily perched on a willow branch. Cowbirds are parasitic nesters, sneaking in their own egg when the rightful nest-owner is away on legitimate business. Sometimes the offended sparrow or warbler will cover up the intruder's egg and lay its own eggs above; sometimes it will abandon the nest entirely. If nothing is done the cowbird fledgling outcompetes the native young, sometimes pushes them out of the nest to death on the ground below, and most often becomes the only fledgling survivor. I was witness to the last act of a sparrow family tragedy.

About midafternoon, noise and smell gave warning of something unpleasant ahead. Five minutes and two meanders later I saw them: a herd of cattle milling about in the shallows in stupefied bewilderment. Their original intention had been to "ford" the river, although that word implies more direction and intelligence than should be associated with these foolish beasts. The river mud unnerved them by sucking at their legs; they turned first one way, then the other, and were further agitated by the appearance of canoe-man. While I backpaddled impatiently, waiting for some resolution to their indecision, the flies, *their* flies, assaulted me. With my legs folded up underneath me, the soles of my feet were naked to enterprising horseflies. One took the opportunity to land unseen and sample a softer, sweeter delicacy than tough cowhide; the sudden removal of a good chunk of the arch in the sole of my right foot meant throbbing pain for an hour afterwards. Adult cowbirds watched the surgical strike with professional curiosity from the riverbank bush. Cowbirds are beneficial in pest control; they often make their living by eating the flies that surround prairie cattle and will sometimes ride on the back of a convenient bovine. In the buffalo era they found abundant flies among the great herds, and were locked in like wolf, grizzly bear, and man to the migration patterns of the buffalo. Here, judging by the swarms of flies around me, the living must be easy, and I supposed that these must be sated cowbirds above me, uninterested in any offer of canoe companionship I might propose.

Eventually, and for no apparent reason, the cattle looking down at me from the starboard bank concluded I was dangerous. They backed away, bellowing, and moved off in an audible, if invisible, shambling stampede. This was enough to alarm those cattle in the river ahead of me into a decision and they struggled in a panicked waddle through to the starboard bank, the muddy bottom tugging sloppily at their hooves. When the way ahead was clear I paddled on quickly, eager to leave flies and stench behind. The bawling continued above and behind me for a quarter of an hour.

Once clear of cattle country, I kept watch for a suitable campsite. I had several siting objectives, foremost of which was a site exposure such that the wind would be strong enough to sweep away mosquitoes, but not so strong as to blow down the tent. A rise above the valley floor was desirable, for it made for a dry pitch and a good view. Preferably there would be a sandbank along the river allowing easy beaching and unloading of the canoe. If I was very lucky I might find a landing with a few rocks rather than just the usual mud and fine sand, for rocks or gravel made it easier to brace the water filter and to scour dirty pans. Finally, as I had learned the hard way on my dog journey, the site had to be free of any livestock, be they horses or cattle.

I paddled another half hour until the river swung up hard against the south wall of the valley. A narrow sandbar appeared below the shoulder of a steep hill. I hesitated briefly, for the bank here was high and nearly vertical, but then turned the canoe sharply and drove it hard onto the sand. It was indeed a tough scramble up the bank, but I was pleased with the site above, a small patch of rich native grass sloping up into dense aspen bush. Its small size and hilly relief had saved this prairie corner from the farmer; it was too rough and isolated for the plough and not large enough to be worth fencing for grazing. The slope was well exposed to the now gusty wind; fortunately the wind direction was constant and I could align the tent in parallel. Should the breeze become stronger still, I could retreat into the shelter of the upslope bush.

Satisfied, I paused to consider the wider domain. Here, elevated above the floodplain, I had a superb view of the sweep of the valley. There were cattle visible below, but far enough away that I could almost imagine them to be nobler animals of an earlier age, although even at great distance their rear ends were too corpulent and their chests too skinny to allow the willing mind to take them for buffalo. This was a site that might reasonably have been used by Indian peoples before me, so I kept an eye out for surface lithics hidden in the thick grass. When the rituals of tent assembly, cooking, eating, and washing-up were completed, I enjoyed a black tea. This was a far more auspicious beginning than my first day of dog travels. The sun was setting behind my left shoulder, pouring clear amber light onto the far valley wall. The wind was abating. On the valley floor below and in front of me cattle hooves dragged over overgrazed pasture, stirring up dust particles that were held suspended by the afternoon's rising heat. The levitated soil shimmered golden around the fat black dots that were cattle. For a moment the valley seemed akin to the Great Rift Valley of Africa: ancient, a place where life might begin, a place to find the footprints of ancestors. It felt good to be alive as I crawled into the tent in search of sleep and dreams.

I awoke just before dawn. So far as possible I dressed to leave no skin exposed before emerging from the tent to brave the morning mosquito frenzy. Under the palest flush of early light I struck the tent quickly. My gear I slid down the bank and stowed forward in the canoe. That done, I was able to push off and stroke hard downriver. In a minute trailing mosquitoes had left me, not to return until the next landfall. Mosquitoes are unhappy over open water, for they are exposed there to swallows, dragonflies, and other predators, while their chances of encountering a meal of warm blood in midlake or midriver are slim. I was profoundly grateful for the daily paddling respite from the biting hordes.

As the morning advanced, fish became obvious basking in the shallows; spearfishing would have been easy work. Twice fish thumped against the bottom of the canoe and startled me, although not so badly as unknown fish, probably catfish, frightened the nervous Jesuit Jacques Marquette during his Mississippi explorations of 1673. He reported fearfully: "From time to time, we came upon monstrous fish, one of which struck our Canoe with such violence that I Thought that it was a great tree, about to break the Canoe to pieces."

Judging by the richness of visible life, the river was healthy. When gliding I could approach muskrat to within a yard. Beaver, too, were not wary and the river was thick with them. I heard the rasping and scraping of one at work inside its bank lodge as I passed by. A sunbathing turtle, about twenty centimetres long, was more watchful, and slipped into the water at my approach. I saw great blue herons often, always alone, and typically at the mouth of a backwater or where a coulee channel joined the river. The heron would rise up with slow dignity and grace, half-circle with folded neck and trailing legs, and then most often would glide down to land some few meanders downstream. In a few minutes the process would repeat itself; the spear-billed hunters seemed unable to grasp the futility of landing ahead of a forward-moving danger. Butterflies were trapped on the water surface around me; with Olympian effort a few managed to break the cruel physics of surface tension and flutter up a centimetre or two, only to fall back again, condemned by waterlogged wings to be recycled into fish. Skimming beetles swarmed at river's edge, mating at speed. It was not quite Arctic urgency, but life in the brief northern prairie summer must also move quickly.

Though Dickinson had complained of "no rest for eye or finger" on the endless river meanders, these turnings did mean the journey was always full of possible discovery. Who knew what might lie beyond the next bend? Dickinson himself had taken some pleasure, detectible even through his restrained Victorian prose, in one unexpected sight, even if he makes "the current," rather than his paddle, responsible for his close approach. In his words: ". . . as we swiftly and noiselessly glided round a sudden bend, we were borne by the current very close indeed to a group of Indian women who were enjoying the pleasures of a bath, quite as much to our astonishment as to theirs. First a loud chorus of screams arose [presumably from the women], and then there was a rushing about for blankets and other apparel, which they adjusted with most wonderful rapidity, and then away they scampered to their wigwams laughing heartily as they went."

While I was still absent-mindedly musing on Dickinson's aesthetic encounter, the canoe rounded a bend and confronted me with a creature quite outside my speculations. It was perched on a fence post that leaned out over the river, the footing undercut by erosion. Frozen in midstroke, I drifted underneath a near eagle-sized mass of black feathers out of which emerged a naked red head suspended two metres over the water on a plumber's trap of a neck. The vulture was, like myself, startled into immobility, until I had drifted so far past that there was no point in flight. Turkey vultures are rare so far north, but had once been common in the northern prairies, making a comfortable living from the natural demise of millions of buffalo yearly. I found the close view disturbing. The river was not just exuberant with life, as I had begun to picture it; it necessarily followed that there must be plenty of death about too, and this river visitor was clearly hoping to sample some.

Later I surprised a pair of sandhill cranes which were standing on a small sandbar on the inside bank of a curve. Though they were over one metre tall, their ruddy colour suggested they were juveniles. Again I could pass close by as they stared at me, confused. Sandhill cranes are not known to nest in the valley, so seeing a pair in midsummer was very unusual. They made an elegant contrast to the vulture.

Some meander discoveries were completely unwelcome. Rounding a curve late in the paddling day, I saw a fence line ahead which crossed the river. I was by now used to this hazard, having already come through six fences without incident. It had been possible to either use the paddle to lift the lowest strand of barbed wire over the canoe or, if the lowest wire was low to the water, to jab it underneath. This latter tactic necessitated moving forward in the canoe, leaning out over the bow, and striking down straight and clean with the paddle blade as momentum and current carried the canoe forward. So far my timing had been accurate.

This particular fence was something new, however, for the wires were electric rather than barbed. The river flowed quickly here, so there was clearly potential for trouble. I considered the situation carefully as I backpaddled. It was more likely than not that the fence was not charged and was therefore harmless. This would certainly be the case if there were no livestock in the pasture. Even if there were cattle or horses about, the fence would only need to be live from time to time to keep them respectful. Of course, I had to assume the fence was charged. The bottom wire hung just high enough over the water that had it been barbed rather than electric I would have opted to lift it over me, but to lift an electric wire would be to run a perhaps unnecessary risk of contact. It seemed safer to try and push the wire underneath the canoe.

I carefully straightened my craft, approached the fence cautiously, and then moved swiftly to the bow. My timing was flawless on the paddle blade strike and the wire plunged down, slid underneath the canoe—and stuck! It was awful luck—the wire was fractionally too taut to allow it to stretch under the canoe. I scrambled astern and backpaddled desperately, for now the craft, pushed by the current, was in danger of swinging broadside into the fence. For a moment, as the canoe slid back off the wire, I thought I was safe, but faster than the eye could follow, the over-stretched wire snapped back up out of the water and for a second caught on the bow tip of the aluminum gunwale. A tremendous jolt wrenched my body—some part of me must have been in contact with the gunwale! The wire rebounded again, free of the bow tip, and I just managed to paddle back and away from the fence. I had actually felt my heart seize in midbeat and my gut was wrenched to the point of vomiting.

I braced and rested along the bank. Queasiness mixed with anger; wire cutters were what I wanted now. But I had none and I still had a problem. It would be difficult to portage the canoe over the fence without touching body or gunwale to wire, and I anyway resented being forced off the water. I determined to try again on the river, this time trying to go under the lowest wire, hard on the port bank, where the current was slower and the wires rose a little higher. Cautiously I pried up the wire and slid it the length of my paddle while lying flat on my back. Toward the stern of the canoe the wire brushed the gunwale, but this time I was safely centered away from any contact. I was through.

I camped on a flat patch of meadow grass not much bigger than my tent, just a metre above the river near the Ellisboro bridge. The nesting cliff swallows were good company and swept away mosquitoes, just as they had done for Serge and me when we passed this way a year ago. It was only a kilometre's walk up to the twin churches and last year's campsite, but now it seemed an impossible distance to traverse for reminiscence's sake. My shoulders ached, and food and rest were the primary needs. I had with me an old-fashioned foam lifejacket, uncomfortable to wear, and far from dependable in boating emergencies, but remarkably useful in ways unintended by the manufacturer. While canoeing, I used it as a knee pad; while resting, as a pillow; and now, while cooking, as a flat base for my little mountaineer's stove. With the meal cooked, the jacket did final service as a kind of Japanese floor table.

With my belly filled, I reflected upon my fence travails, my Canadianized mind searching for a reasonable compromise. It was illegal for a landholder to block a navigable waterway, whatever his or her practical needs. But this would not help me here in farm country; when I pictured myself trying to win the sympathy of a jury of Saskatchewan farmers, I laughed. I concluded that I could accept barbed wire fences, so long as they were clearly visible (they would be safer if red-flagged) and not strung across a rapids. But I would happily cut any electric fence, given the chance. Satisfied with my work as advocate, judge, and jury, I got a solid sleep with the babble of the riffle below masking the frenetic buzz of night-time mosquitoes dancing above the tent. It was not the last time I would have reason to think about fences.

Next morning I was packed and on the water a full hour before sunrise. It was a cool 12° C, perfect for paddling, and so calm that in the dawning light I could watch the river bubbles float unbroken round the bends, fast along the cut-bank curve, slow along the inside curve. At times the river appeared to split—if there was no discernible current, as was the case in some reaches, it was hard to detect the true channel and avoid entering a waterway to nowhere. The bubbles often gave a clue to the right course to follow, but as the wind rose the water surface riffled and became a riddle to read. Once I chose the wrong route and found myself losing energy up a dead-end meander. The error cost me about a half hour's paddling, but I did not regret the detour, for it brought me to a colony of bank swallows. White-fronted with a dark chest band, they were elegant birds, popping nimbly in and out of their nest holes burrowed into a steep sandy bank.

For an expert observer the flight path of each swallow species is diagnostic. I had rarely seen bank swallows before, so here was a chance to watch carefully. The glides looked shorter and the flight pattern more irregular than for other swal-lows, but I doubted that I could separate them out if mixed with a flight of their swallow cousins. They did not seem much bothered by my presence on the water and sometimes swept very close to the canoe, chittering softly all the while.

When I returned to the true channel I found the wind had strengthened enough to drive whitecaps down east-west reaches of the river. The bank wil-lows whipped over the water, moaning softly. With the wind came ragged flotillas of fair-weather cumuli driven eastward parallel to the general line of the valley. There were clouds both to the north and to the south of the valley, but above the valley proper the sky remained clear. It was a classic weather phenomenon: the south-facing slopes, heated by the sun, were generating an updraft that sucked in air from across the valley floor. A downdraft into the valley completed the circula-tion cell and explained both the cloudless blue directly above me and the relative strength of the valley wind compared with the slower drift of the clouds.

The ceaseless windings of the river ensured that I got plenty of paddling downwind, upwind, and broadside to the gusts. Stroking upwind was good fun, for although it was hard work, its duration was limited; soon came the reward of another river turn and a wind-push downstream. The variety of strokes required to paddle at all angles to the wind made my work more interesting than it would have been on a straight haul.

As the wind grew loud enough to mask the noise of even the sloppiest canoeist, it became easier to catch river regulars unawares. Horses standing at river's edge froze and stared in midchew before running off cross-country with the blades and culms of grass hanging from their lips. Farther on I approached a mule deer and escaped notice until within thirty metres. He moved off without panic, slowly and deliberately, with the peculiar springing mulie gait. It resembled the stotting performance of an African Thomson's gazelle, conveying a message of personal fitness and implying an ability to escape any chase. If convinced by the brisk, bouncing step of a stot, a prospective predator will look elsewhere for a meal, sparing hunter and hunted the energy cost of a pointless pursuit. But the stot is of no use against a rifle.

Later I sighted a coyote along the bank. He spotted me at a great distance, circled away, and returned to river's edge behind me. With his big ears flared, he watched me disappear downriver. He was grey, with none of the ruddy tones of the earlier coyote, and was more cautious than fearful.

As the day progressed I drank large quantities of water to pre-empt any risk of dehydration. A consequence of high water consumption and hard labor is increased urine production. Urine colour changes, too, to a darker yellow or brownish hue as the body works overtime to rid itself of the waste products of heavy exercise. This colour change can serve as a useful warning to increase water intake, but it was the frequency and urgency of the need to void that emerged as a primary problem. This critical aspect of canoe logistics is addressed neither by master technicians like Bill Mason nor by spiritual devotees like Pierre Trudeau. Yet the problem is as old as the canoe itself. Writing in 1637, Father Paul Le Jeune advised his fellow Jesuits not to complain when travelling with Huron paddlers who sometimes urinated into the same vessels later used for cooking. Despite determined research, I have been unable to find any indication of what was standard voyageur practice. However, from personal experience I can report that it is perfectly possible to pee, without incident, over the side of a slowly moving canoe on flat water. Although there are other male options, this is best done while standing in the stern. Of course, I cannot condone such an environmentally unethical practice, but it was a useful skill to master, given the frequency of its relevance. Besides, as it was never without risk, it added a frisson of excitement to an otherwise mundane activity. Successful completion of nautical micturition never failed to give me juvenile satisfaction. In a lighter-spirited age I might advance my experimental results as incontrovertible evidence that only males can be truly great canoeists, but in modern times there is always the danger of being taken seriously.

By midafternoon the sun was causing me problems. The temperature was only 22° C, but the water reflected the sun's full power back in my face. I was well covered up, even to the point of wearing thin cotton gloves, for my Scottish ancestors have bequeathed me a pale skin, sadly vulnerable to the prairie sun. Yet despite my best precautions I was developing an exposure headache. I kept a sharp eye out for a suitable campsite, but the central valley bottomlands where the river now meandered were too exposed for comfort. Finally, the river changed course and swung hard up against the north valley wall, cutting into the hillslopes. These south-facing slopes were sun-dried and open, and so had been fenced for pasture. As far as I could tell by looking up from the river, the pasture was empty; cattle would likely be moved in later in the year. I beached the canoe on a sandbar and, before trying to clamber up the steep bank for a reconnaissance, enjoyed a cooling swim in the river, followed by a rest on the sandbar, followed by another swim. Glass, barbed wire, and assorted other garbage can make the river risky to swim in, but swim you can, if you are sensible about where you do it. This spot, distant from bridges, road access, buildings, and fencing, was very probably safe. A good thing, too, for on this and some later afternoons, I simply had to swim in the river to cool down.

Rejuvenated, I scrambled up the bank and confirmed the current absence of cattle, although there were plenty of last year's dried cow pies about. I wondered how good a fire cattle dung would make. I had experienced a buffalo dung fire (*bois de vache* was standard fuel in the old prairie days) and had been impressed by its smokeless, even heat; buffalo dung burns hotter and longer than many a wood fire. Buffalo dung was once plentiful too; Hind even discovered a half-metre stratum of buffalo manure one metre below ground level, exposed in the banks of the Souris River. I doubted cattle dung would be of equal quality and, not wanting to draw attention to myself with an open fire, was not going to experiment here.

I pitched tent on a grassy rise high above the river with a good view of the valley. This time I had the sun in front of me. It obscured my view of landscape detail, but the soft-hued beauty of a summer sunset filtered and splintered through rising valley humidity was full compensation. In the slow-fading light I could make out a beaver in the river below. He swam to the same sandbar that I had dozed on and spent several minutes snuffling and scratching at traces of man-scent before moving on to his normal evening business. Several other beaver joined him; for no apparent reason they sometimes slapped their tails and dove underwater in short-lived alarm. Unless my lingering scent had disturbed them, their nervousness had nothing to do with me, for I was quiet, some distance away, and downwind of them.

It was a peaceful moment in a peaceful place, a good time for reflection. What had most surprised me so far was the richness and diversity of river life; I had seen far more wildlife on the Qu'Appelle than I would expect to see while paddling the northern woodland lakes and rivers. Any disappointments or troubles I had so far encountered had been man-made. Tomorrow I would be meeting my paddling partner, Rob, who was to accompany me for the next five days. I would be giving up the landscape intimacy of solo canoeing for the sharing of insights and for the pleasure of good company. It was an even bargain. A weak thunderstorm, spinning cotton-candy wisps of gentle rain ahead of a massing nimbus, was slowly rolling down-valley from the west, just like those that Hind reported as frequent in the valley. The light was almost gone when, fully content, I crawled in to sleep just as the storm's first squall shook the tent.

In next dawn's hazy light the air was humid and still. Beaver tails slapped in all directions as I pushed off onto the river with a pale sun edging over the horizon. The haze-refracted light, and the mist rising from the water, wove a dreamy, soothing spell that nearly proved my undoing, for lost in the pleasing dazzle of reflections was a solitary fence wire strung casually across the river. As I squinted down an east-facing reach I saw it at the last second and only narrowly avoided being garroted. Shaken, I remained *en garde* until the mist burnt off and the sun angle improved. The sky then clouded over and the next three hours of paddling were uneventful. Rob was waiting for me at a river bridge.

It took some time to redistribute the new gear and Rob's weight in my small canoe. Because Rob was considerably heavier than I was it proved impossible to level the canoe; one end was going to have to ride a bit higher than the other. This is not ideal, but is less serious if it is the stern that sits slightly deeper, which meant that Rob would have to paddle there for the duration of our joint venture. I was happy to leave the "high privilege," as I called it, of sterning to Rob in exchange for my superior view as bowman. More work for him on this twisty river! In voyageur tradition the *gouvernail*, the stern or steersman, was the best paid of canoeists, receiving for his skill and responsibility roughly double the pay of the humble *milieu*, the midshipman. I myself as *devant*, or bowman, had extra responsibility as well, and could expect *gouvernail* wages, or slightly less. Given the interminable turning work that lay ahead, the grumbles that rose from a malcontent steersman behind me were forgivable.

Although we abandoned voyageur wage scales, in one worrying sense we maintained tradition. With the added weight of Rob plus his gear, our freeboard was reduced to, or even slightly below, the risky minimum of six inches maintained by the fully loaded north canoes of old. We would have to be cautious, especially on the lake traverses ahead, at least until we shed some collective weight. My steersman listened stony-faced to these concerns, then pushed us cleanly away from the bank. We were off and powering smoothly underneath the bridge. A large colony of cliff swallows, disturbed from their nests, flew out ahead us, an expanding cloud of wings. It was an auspicious start.

For a time we conversed. Rob had the advantage of speaking forwards, while I had the advantage when listening; intra-canoe communication has a one-way bias. But soon we fell silent to the rhythm of team paddling, which, owing to the extra weight in the canoe and endless turnings of the river, proved to be no faster than solo paddling. As we slid by the banks I could see the spring flood waterline about half a metre above the present river level. Looking ahead over a sandbar and through thin willow, I caught sight of a curious juxtaposition of land uses: an old farm garbage dump slumped into the water beside a private graveyard similarly threatened by fluvial erosion. Intrigued, we beached the canoe to explore. The graveyard was some fifty or sixty metres square, but contained only seven graves. They lay tightly grouped in a corner, unbalancing the site. Had there been expectations of many future burials from families since moved on? Had the same optimism been at work that led prairie town leaders to build immensely broad main streets? As for garbage beside graves—perhaps there was a kind of logic in placing those goods and bodies beyond worldly use close together. What clearly did not belong together were the river and the dump. It depressed me to think how easily this could have been avoided. I had seen bits of barbed wire, tractor tires, plastic, broken concrete, phosphate foam, and now a full garbage dump itself in the river. The pollution was not surprising, for we have used rivers as the sewers of civilizations for millennia. But the Qu'Appelle was, on the whole, cleaner than most watercourses, and I wanted to keep it that way.

Late in the afternoon we pulled up at Hyde, where Serge and I had rested the previous summer after crossing through the bush and wetlands just to the west. As then, the site was deserted. There was a clear view across the valley, the spring provided good water, and there were plenty of mature trees for shade. A striking tree-lined approach road, resembling an old European allée, led to an abandoned farmhouse. The house, too unwieldy for conversion to modern heating and too large for modern families, was quietly decaying. Around it were scattered bits of fence and odds and ends of farm equipment. The atmosphere, as around many deserted prairie homesteads, was both peaceful and melancholic.

Rob and I talked late into the evening. I spoke of my first days on the river and we sketched out a canoeing plan for those to come. Our "business" complete, Rob related stories from the "real world" beyond the valley, accounts of his work with governments and bureaucracies. The characters and settings were modern, but the story lines were ancient parables of intrigue and ambition whose lineage reached back beyond even the schemings of pharaohs' scribes in the pyramid-building campaigns; indeed, in age and sinuosity Rob's modern narratives rivaled the fourteen-thousand-year-old Qu'Appelle itself. For a time I forgot river and valley entirely as we joked contentedly of government-boondoggles-I-have-known. But when Rob stood up to move to his tent for the night's rest his tall frame threw a block of blackness against the starry night and remembrance of time and place present flooded back. Alone in the darkness, it seemed as if the stillness of the valley wrapped itself around me and spoke: "Speak not here of human ambition and foolishness; rather be silent, and reflect on grass, river, stars, and wind."

The next morning we launched in near darkness. It was overcast and too warm for dew. Two great horned owls watched us glide underneath their roost in a riverbank tree. Owls seem otherworldly at any time (most every culture ascribes some preternatural characteristics to them), but in the predawn light these were odd-looking birds indeed; they looked huge, white, and, most impossibly, hairy.

Throughout the paddling day an east wind strengthened. The valley flattened and opened as we approached Crooked Lake and both riverbanks declined to mere levees, offering little shelter from the wind. Although technically blowing against our line of travel, more often the wind hit us broadside as the river swung in great north-south loops back and forth across the valley. We were paddling through a vast delta region where only the low levees separated us from swamp and marsh country. Somewhere in this world of fermenting mud and reed was a patch of solid pasture, for we could hear cattle bawling in the distance. As there was no evident cause for bovine concern, we concluded that they were complaining about taxes.

When one of the great river loops brought us hard up against the north valley wall and then turned sharply back to the south, jumbled broken concrete that had been dumped over the cut bank aroused our suspicions. We landed and climbed onto the rubble to inspect. Only ten metres to the east was the river again, returned from its umpteenth visit to the far side of the valley. The amateur revetment we were standing on was doubtless the work of a local landholder. Left to itself, the river would erode through this narrow neck of land and the landholder would lose this access to his or her bottomland pasture. The erosive force of the current cannot be eliminated, merely shunted elsewhere (as Americans have discovered at great expense on the Mississippi), so the next downstream cut bank of the Qu'Appelle would be eroding a little faster.

We were not about to confirm this hydrological hypothesis, for by portaging here we could save at least three kilometres of north-south paddling. The time required to unload, move, and repack all our gear in the canoe meant that ultimately we saved neither time nor energy, but it was good to get out on land and to stretch stiffened muscles. As we stood exposed on the barren isthmus, the wind whipped about us. Portage complete, we were happy to drop back down a few feet to the half-shelter of the river.

A few windings later even the low levees fell away and we paddled a sinuous path through a sea of reed that bent and sighed with the wind. There was no discernible current and the tall reed blocked our vision; only the wind and the sun gave some inkling of direction. We knew that the river does not arrive modestly at the edge of Crooked Lake, but instead spreads its grand reed delta far out into the greater waters. This was unfortunate, for we would pass from shelter to the full force of offshore conditions with no safe shoreline to retreat to. We knew, too, we would have to paddle against the wind for a long eastward reach, and we had had plenty of time to speculate on the height of the waves that would face us. Above all, we were acutely aware of our minimal freeboard.

Sure enough, the river ended abruptly in an expanse of wind-tossed white-caps. After five days in an intimate river landscape, the lake looked vast—an impression that strengthened as, for stability's sake, I hunkered lower in the bow.

Ahead of us, extending from the north shore of the lake, was a point that promised shelter behind its leeward flank, but to reach it would require an open water traverse of about a kilometre. We had a choice of either chancing the crossing or of retreating far back up the river in search of solid ground, with the intent of sitting out the night in mosquito country and awaiting better wind conditions. Uncertain, we edged out cautiously from the river's mouth. Whack!—I took a shot of spray in the face. Rob angled the canoe to port to quarter the waves and voiced the opinion, "We could probably make it." I agreed, "We probably could," given a confident steersman and a full head of steam. And on these weak premises we set off, our doubts rising and falling with the waves and spray.

We paddled hard to the northeast, cutting the waves at the safest angle possible, 30° as viewed from the stern (the cut angle can look significantly different seen from the bow, but the steersman's judgment rules). I was quickly soaked by flying spray and, although uneasy, enjoyed this full employ of muscles to a single purpose. "Now this is canoeing!" I thought, as our little boat plunged and rose and the spray flew white around us, flecking the world with foam. But, behind me, the confidence of the wise old man of the sea was being eroded by a deepening pool of water beneath him; Rob knew the stern was dropping and so took a few crucial seconds from paddling to buckle his gear to the thwarts. There had been no need for such precautions on the river, but in our current situation it was a wise move which, as he carefully related to me afterwards, he had judged it best not to mention at the time, so as not to "damage crew morale." I knew nothing of the cool calculations going on astern, exhilarated as I was by rollicking wave and slashing blade, and foolishly emboldened by the fact that the bow still rode as high as ever. Our minimal freeboard was proving our undoing.

There can be glory in a failed river rapids run, but only ignominy in a midlake swamping. The crisis came when we had to turn across the waves to tack into the lee of the point. With the extra weight dragging on the stern, the canoe was sluggish on the turn; we took a heavy wave and, for a terrible moment, it seemed we had lost all momentum and were done for. Adrenalin must have surged in us both

Crossing Crooked Lake

as we realized how close to sinking we were, for we managed to recover, power forward, and, after a few minutes of anaerobic desperation, limp into calmer waters. We grounded on the sands of the point with the canoe reduced to half its earlier freeboard. We were laughing and joking as we stepped on shore, as our adrenalin rush mixed with the light-headed, witless euphoria people experience when they know they have just gotten away with something foolish. I was as relieved to set foot again on solid ground as Serge must have felt at the end of his stressful river crossing of a year ago. Rob carefully explained how *my* gear bag he had left unbuckled to a thwart, as he had thought it so heavy that "it would have sunk the canoe and we would have lost everything." His logic was impeccable and there was nothing left for me to do but to acknowledge his level head and good judgment.

We unloaded our gear and drained the canoe. Some of our equipment was wet, but the essential gear had been double-bagged and was still dry. We took a stroll on the point and then crossed over to the opposite side to view the water conditions. It was apparent we had negotiated the roughest reach of open water and it looked safe to proceed farther, hugging close to the north shore, where we could quickly take shelter in the event of any difficulty. And so we continued slowly down the lake, a relieved, more cautious, but also triumphant pair of canoeists.

Despite its choppiness, the lake water was green with filamentous algae and in places weedy as well. This growth is essentially natural in all the valley lakes, although amplified by domestic sewage and farm fertilizer runoff. On his paddle through Katepwa Lake, Dickinson complained: "For three miles we passed through a dense decaying mass of confervæ, which an east wind had driven to the upper parts of the lake. The smell of it was most unpleasant; the men pushed through it as hard as they could, no easy matter, as it impeded the progress of the canoe considerably." For us, too, the east wind and thick water made for heavy paddling and it took an hour and a half of toil before we made landfall at Crooked Lake Provincial Park near the east end of the lake.

The park was once called "Last Oak," for this is where the westbound voyageur last saw the bur oak, a tree common in the valley to the east. After the retreat of the last continental ice sheet, the light seeds of maple, elm, and ash were blown hither and thither across the prairie to grow where conditions allowed, but the acorn is a heavy seed moved only by animal or water. Since prairie rivers flow unhelpfully west to east, the oaks' progress has been slow, creeping westward up-valley from the deciduous woods of southeastern Manitoba in the millennia since the ice left the prairies. You might hope that a name like "Last Oak," resonant with both fur trader history and ecological insight, would be treasured. You would hope in vain. Years ago the park was renamed after the lake to simplify matters for the tourist.

Whatever its name, we were thankful to arrive at the park. Some of the campsites back onto the lakeshore, which allowed us the luxury of inspecting them from the water and then beaching at the one we most liked the look of. We pulled the canoe well up out of the water, then pitched tents and snoozed before inspecting campground comforts. Drinking water, as much as you liked, at the turn of a tap—after a mere five days of pumping and filtering it seemed like a minor miracle. And there was more: shelter, a small store and cafe, flush toilets, and one of humanity's few indisputably great inventions, the hot shower. With renewed appreciation we enjoyed the daily comforts of the rich industrial world.

Yet, as much as I valued the physical conveniences at this lakeside portal of Western civilization, I was eager for tomorrow's journey and the rewards of travel in the natural valley. With decent weather and an early start we could cover the fifty-odd kilometres to Round Lake. Having been lucky today on Crooked Lake, I went to sleep awash in prairie optimism.

I woke at earliest light to the restless sounds of creaking trees and slapping water. I listened for a few minutes, then left my tent to survey the lake. The wind had swung round to the west and was blowing at gale-force strength. Great white-caps rolled down from the far end of the lake. Under a somber sky, heavy with low grey cloud, the water was dark and colorless. I retreated to the tent and to a light sleep, but when after several hours I re-emerged, conditions had not improved. Under a greenish-grey North Atlantic light the waves roiled far too rough for canoeing. The first of the day's many rainsqualls rolled down-valley into my face. For the second time I retreated to the tent and zipped down the flysheet.

The English have a simple plan for such days (which are, after all, not so unusual in their country): many cups of tea. Tea became the framework around which the whole day was structured: reading, then tea; cribbage, then tea; walking, then tea; cooking and eating, then tea. The black brew we were drinking had also been basic to the voyageurs' progress. They consumed it liberally whenever they found themselves grounded by wind. Stranding had been most feared when paddling the length of Lake Winnipeg, a key link between Montreal and the Northwest, for the lake is immense and the passage long and exposed. Usually the voyageurs canoed along the lake's western shoreline. If they were lucky and met with the prevailing westerlies, there was little problem, but if strong easterlies developed they were sometimes stranded for a week or more. Happily there was little danger of us being marooned so long at Crooked Lake, and I determined to profit from the enforced layover by reading the old traders' narratives.

These journals brought home that, while we had tea aplenty, we were missing the voyageurs' second great solace, pipe tobacco. Tobacco was so important to the voyageurs that it came to underlie the most civilized unit of measurement yet devised, the "pipe." All satisfying measures, like the foot or the furlong, are based on some aspect of human scale or endeavour, but only the pipe is grounded in relaxation. During the brief rest breaks allowed the voyageurs, they invariably enjoyed a reviving smoke, and the name "pipe" came to denote the work interval between rest stops. Although it took both into account, after some study I conclude that a pipe was a fixed span of neither time nor distance, for these two dimensions varied with the direction of travel (up or downstream) and the time of year and strength of current. Thus a spring downstream journey might cover thirty kilometres in three hours, require no portages, and rate as a journey of two pipes. The much more demanding upstream return journey in autumn might require three portages and eight hours, and rate as ten pipes. A pipe was really a rough measure of energy output—the modern and inelegant equivalents are joules or calories.

Dickinson had enjoyed good weather when he camped at Crooked Lake, or *Kawawak-kamac*, as he recorded it in Cree. In my rain-soaked tent I at least had the benefit of his view from valley's edge at sunset:

I need not try to describe the exceeding beauty of the scene, for I could not; I will merely state what the components of the picture were. The sun just merged from behind a bank of crimson clouds reflected in the waters of Crooked Lake; part of the valley in deep shade and part brightly illuminated. The vivid green of the young poplars on one side, and on the other large granite boulders lying on the bare and rugged surface of the slope. The blue smoke of the wigwams rising up high and straight from the bottom of the valley. The river, with its complicated coils, gliding among the willow bushes. To the south the great prairie, ocean-like, with its many islands of aspens and single trees, looking in the distance, and by twilight, like becalmed ships. As this view just dissolves away, another rises very pleasant to see,—our camp fire is now burning brightly below.

Late in the morning a kind-hearted camper offered to drive our canoe and gear down to the end of the lake, from where we could launch onto the river, avoiding the lake's heaving whitecaps entirely. This would have been against the spirit of our journey, so we declined and awaited a break in the weather. But the rain and wind held steady. It was instructive that wind was such a constraint on our water-bound progress. Just as it had been necessary to be acutely aware of temperature when travelling with Serge, it was now necessary to be conscious of wind. Other characteristics of our journey were its downstream bias and the need to be aware of the shape of the land and the water flows that result from particular terrains. Understanding the constraints and opportunities imposed by the freeze-thaw cycle and high and low water conditions is also important to canoeists. I liked the way such environmental realities forced me to be in touch with the landscape and weather around me.

The day wore on. When I was hungry, I ate, and when I was tired, I slept, letting my body slide into a primordial rhythm driven only by immediate bodily needs. On such a dull day I was grateful my fellow paddler remained full of good humour, untroubled by delay or bad weather. Eventually, outside the tent, day gloom shaded into night darkness.

Next morning dawned as if made for canoeing. There was cloud still, but suspended high above us; the air was swept of mist and fog, and the prairie world had re-expanded to its natural bounds. A diminished west wind pushed us down to the end of the lake, where we found a weir like that at Katepwa. After a short portage we relaunched downriver. Yesterday's heavy rains had raised water levels everywhere and the keen wind had driven much water over the weir, so we enjoyed a strong current downstream to Round Lake. The high cloud cover held all day, shielding us from the prairie sun, and the occasional passing shower served only to cool us. It was an especially fortuitous combination of circumstances, for today's journey was longer than any previous. We praised the canoe gods.

To port a marsh harrier quartered low over the valley floor, rising, tail coverts flashing white, then sinking out of sight. Farther on there was rustling in the riverbanks ahead. We feathered the paddles. Two thin brown bodies arched and looped in and out of the tangled grass. They were stalking in tandem, one to each riverbank, synchronizing their hunt with cross-river squeals. They were mink, lithe and quick, and every body movement emanated predatory efficiency. We watched, fascinated, until one of them noticed us, gave a single high-pitched shriek, and they vanished up and over the banks.

Mink are common in the valley. Once, out walking a valley trail, I had heard scrambling in the bush a yard to my right. The noises see-sawed mysteriously back and forth on a line parallel to the path, but hidden by undergrowth. Finally I caught a fleeting glimpse of mink. Clearly it was hunting something—but what? The hidden frantic scuffling continued another minute. Suddenly a field mouse emerged onto the edge of the trail, hesitated, and then in a desperate half-second of mouse-time eternity made a life-saving decision. Its tiny legs sprang, fairly rocketing it across the path, right over the toe of my left boot and into the far-side grass. On my right the snuffling continued for about another ten seconds until a weasel-like hunter's head lunged out from the undergrowth. The mink took a single step to cross the trail in pursuit, then froze in shock at my sight and smell. The twist back into cover was almost too fast to follow, but the shriek of frustration and anger that rose from deep within the bush was clear and chilling.

We reached the northwest shore of Round Lake in the early afternoon. The river ended abruptly at lake's edge; there was no delta to navigate as there had been at Crooked Lake. An hour of steady stroking along the north shore, safe in the lee of the strengthening northwest wind, brought us to Bird's Point. Here was the small cafe where last September with Serge I had been so grateful for coffee and shelter from wind, rain, and snow. Bird's Point, like most all points in the valley lakes, owes its origin to a coulee running far back into the valley hills and surrounding plain. Some millennia ago the coulee creek swept silt and gravel down from the hills and into the lake, where the push of prevailing wind and current shouldered the alluvium eastward and sculpted the point into an east-leaning arc. Beyond the tip of the point a ridge of gravel extends underwater until it too makes a final curl to the east and drops off into deeper waters.

Last of the valley lakes, Round Lake, or *Ka-wa-wi-ga-kamac* in Cree as recorded by Dickinson, is perhaps also the most beautiful. There is a little more rain in the eastern valley, so the south-side slopes are thicker with trees. The hills are more rounded than those to the west, and the lake seems to rest a little deeper in the valley. A few summer cottages are scattered along the point and the north shore. The south shore and topland are part of Indian Reserve number 71, *Ochapowace*. Treaty negotiations often landed Native peoples with those tracts thought to be of least interest to white settlers, such as the steep bush land I could see across the lake and the scrub land that I knew extended above it to the south. But, occasionally and unreliably, fate brings justice. With the rise and rise of leisure, wooded waterfront land is now prized by cottage dwellers. A few Indian reserves now benefit from this irony by leasing out cottage land.

We arose at dawn and launched into a morning as calm as the Buddha. Around us polished water lay heavy in a silent lake. It seemed a sacrilege to split the water's flawless surface with blade and bow. Shock waves and ripples expanded around us. Yet the waters healed behind us and perfection returned to the world.

At lake's end two weirs stood fully open, with water roaring through. The portage was straightforward and we pushed on downstream at a good pace. The river was running very high and I could see no trace of a higher spring season watermark. The meanders were small, quite unlike the great valleyside-to-valleyside sweeps of the river above Crooked Lake, but they were also never-ending, demanding Rob's full attention to constant course correction. As the sun rose above the hills and swept the valley with bright morning splendor, the scene was set for disaster.

For the last three days I had seen no cross-river fence wires and had almost forgotten their existence. Lost in the sun, it was only at the very last moment that I noticed an ambush laid with the guile of Satan, a single strand strung low over the water and running from bush into bush without a riverbank fence post to alert the eye. Even as I shouted "Wire!" our momentum and the strong current swept us into contact. I lunged forward and made a desperate stab with my blade. I struck home and the wire plunged under the bow, scraped underneath the canoe, and then tensed and held us amidship. All within a second the current swung us broadside and we were hung up, tilted upstream, and taking on a riverful of fast-flowing water. In a second more we were completely swamped. Its work apparently done, the wire groaned and released us downstream. Submerged in flowing water, we paddled heavily to shore. There we removed our gear and drained the canoe. Everything emerged safely from immersion; we had lost nothing but pride, for which we compensated by free-form cursing.

At the second of three further wire encounters we had to line the canoe along the shoreline through a narrow gap in the fence. Leeches aplenty had taken mouthholds on the stony riverbed, a rare habitat in a river of sand and silt. As we splashed through the shallows they clung eagerly to flesh. It made me queasy to pull at the bloodsuckers; their bodies had a horrible glutinous texture and they stretched and shrivelled unnervingly. We lined the canoe a second time at an artificial ford built to connect the two sides of a now-abandoned farmstead. It was a beautiful site to stretch the legs and relax. The jumbled rocks made good seats for lunch and the river foamed and chattered as it hurried over the lip of the ford. Around us the grass, silent, green, and rich, stretched higher to the sun god.

Farther downstream the river was rich with waterfowl. Dickinson had reported: "Ducks and geese crowded the river for several miles; there were enough of them, I should think, to supply all the markets in Canada." It was a fanciful exaggeration, but I could understand his amazement at the wealth of birds. Herons rose from nearly every creek estuary or dead-end meander mouth. Ducks were everywhere; especially common were blue-winged teal. With the family well hidden in the tall fringing reed or in backwaters of huge scentless water lilies, many a foolish duck lost her head and shot out into the river to indulge in a broken wing act, long after we were past the relevant hideout. This was a trivial error, for the young remained safe, but whenever we surprised a duck with ducklings in midriver it was difficult to avoid precipitating a family disaster. A few open-water flotillas kept their collective heads, turned sharply, and silently vanished in disciplined tight formation into the reed banks, but more often the ducklings scattered to the four winds and the panicked mother alternated between frantic broken wing displays and desperate attempts to regroup the family, never persisting long enough with either strategy to achieve anything. I fear we contributed to the demise of several ducklings, either hopelessly lost to the mother or victim of hungry river and riverbank predators.

Deer became frequent as well. Most often we only heard them crashing through the bush that lined the riverbanks, but sometimes we caught sight of them. Once we surprised a doe drinking from the river. She lifted her head, confused, nose twitching in vain to catch the scent of the downwind intruders. Later a magnificent whitetail buck stared at us over the sighing reeds, strips of velvet hanging from his antlers.

Of all river life that day the most remarkable were the iridescent blue dragonflies suspended all around and above us. I had never seen so many. Dragonfly populations are cyclical; they often peak a year or two after high mosquito numbers. There are over fifty species native to the prairies, but these were all kinsmen, huge and majestic, keeping silent, even pace with the canoe. Their deep streamlined thoraxes set with stiff double wings and their disciplined formation flying, neat horizontal layers of aviators stacked vertically one above another, put me in mind of a World War II heavy bomber squadron full of dread intent. But happily there were no enemy cities ahead, and no Lancaster or Halifax had the grace of these voracious killers.

Surrounded as we were by natural wonder, it was a shock when the river wound into stocked cattle pasture. I had come to hate these fields with their stench and flies, their fences and muddy, hoof-chopped riverbanks, their fouled water and broken bush. Even the bellowing of cattle was an irritant—mindless noise pollution compared to the spirited complaints of the magpie or kingfisher, the sharp warning snort of the whitetail, or the intelligence and intent audible in the calls of mink, hawk, or coyote. On a long walk in the Arizona desert hills conservationist Edward Abbey spoke with relief at advancing beyond cattle country: "Only one animal remains conspicuous in this region, by its absence—the cow. How delightful it is to walk for mile after mile without encountering the dung, the filth, the heavy tracks, the overgrazed devastation, the swarms of flies, the bovine faces and shambling forms of those gregarious brutes."

It is deeply imbedded in prairie culture that farming and ranching are in some mysterious way good for the land. The implication is that without "good stewardship" the prairie could not survive, that left to itself nature would not be up to the challenge of sustaining a Plains ecology. This is utter nonsense, but the fallacy does allow us to advance our self-interests and to rationalize our resource-extractive prairie lifestyle. The doctrine of the necessity of active land management also serves as a defence mechanism to suppress the remembrance of just how magnificent and self-sustaining the prairies were before we came to section, quarter, and plough them. Prairie city dweller and farmer alike are guilty of the deception of benign occupation. We "reclaim" land, as if it had once been ours, and wheat its natural state. In our worst moments we actually boast of "improving" the prairies—as if they needed it! Nor is the rancher innocent, for while it is true that good ranching practice is far less damaging to natural ecosystems than is the plough of the farmer, it is also true that few individuals have altered more land to their own ends than have ranchers. They have substituted species, changed grazing regimes, and strung thousands of kilometres of barbed wire across the subjugated prairies.

We pitched camp that afternoon next to a community hall in the lowest slopes of the north-side hills. Lounging on sturdy homemade deck chairs and screened from the sun by a broad awning, we enjoyed a comfortable view across the valley. The hills here were rolling back; the valley was broader and softer. Bur oaks, hung with deep-hued leaves, grew all around us on the dry south-facing slopes; their twisted, knotty branches were ideal for hanging up equipment and clothing still wet from the morning's misadventure. Their contorted profile made the young oaks look like stunted victims of some plague of arboreal leprosy, but the larger trees were embodiments of endurance and wisdom. The oaks grew well spaced, with thick grass between them, giving the whole slope an open, savannahlike feel.

It turned out that the hall was privately owned. By chance, late in the afternoon, the owner appeared, and with him containers of fresh water. He donated a gallon to us, which was much appreciated, for it spared us tedious pumping and filtering in the river below. Better still, he regaled us with local gossip. The provincial government, he claimed, had been deliberately releasing extra water from Round Lake to flood out bottomland farmers downstream, who would then be forced to sell out to the government at a bargain price. It was a malevolent vision. The talk shifted and we listened carefully when he told of drinking Qu'Appelle River water while ice fishing with a friend. He and his companion had thought hard about the risk, but the winter water looked so cold and pristine below the ice that they concluded there could be no harm in drinking a half-cup each. Some twenty-four hours later they were both moaning in pain, feeling as if they had been "kicked in the gut." His language was anyway expressive, but just to be sure we got the point he bent over double and tightened his face muscles, miming spasms. Whatever they had suffered, it was likely not giardia, which has a one-week incubation period. Silently I gave thanks for the efficiency of the Swiss and their compact water filter; its high price now seemed cheap.

We launched next morning into a dense river mist. The shrouded passage evoked ambiguity of place and time; mysterious shapes emerged from the banks, approached the edge of cognition, and then faded back into the unknowable behind us. The stink of cattle ahead broke the magic. Slowly the mist lifted to reveal the too-familiar details of a bovine landscape. We paddled on, subdued. Finally the river picked up speed, swung hard into the slope woods lining the south valley wall, and changed character completely. To starboard the bank rose as a vertical cliff, sometimes ten or twelve metres high. There were cheerful rapids where the river had recently engineered a cut-through and abandoned a great meander. The water bounced with the youthful exuberance of a mountain stream; indeed, it was as if we were running some Alberta or Montana foothills torrent. Then the river turned back to the centre of the valley, slowed, and changed character yet again. Now it was a stately marshlands waterway, winding gracefully through thick reed and willow. The luxuriance of growth was astonishing, almost tropical. Green walls rose and arched over us, confining our vision to the river; we were moving through a living tunnel of phloem and xylem with a ragged blue slash of sky above. Ducks were everywhere and deer crashed unseen through the bush around us. Water gurgled and seeped away through low porous banks and into the surrounding marshes. It was as if we had entered some trackless delta swamp—certainly without a boat we would have been hopelessly trapped here. Twice we grounded on a sandbar and stretched up in vain for a view. It was a strange thing on the Plains to lose all sense of open space, to be lost in water and overshadowed by rich vegetation. The world was Carboniferous.

A few kilometres on, dry prairie re-emerged around us and our broad valley vision was restored. Above us, to port, we passed by an abandoned stone farmhouse. Greco-Roman pilasters had been affixed to the corners to give the structure gravitas, but the result was more humorous than effective. Far better to leave honest fieldstone to speak for itself.

Our landing at the village of Tantallon was difficult: there was no convenient sandbar and the riverbanks were steep. We scrambled awkwardly up the port bank. From the river it was a short trek to the community campground. Sadly the campground backs not onto the river proper but instead onto an old oxbow lake, a stagnant pool of rank growth beloved of mosquitoes. There were no other campers—by local accounts the normal state of affairs. At $4.00 a night, showers included, it seemed a bargain. Later my opinion would change.

Rob pitched his tent and crawled in to catch some shut-eye. His journey was now over and, with his further transport arranged, he could sleep with the peace of those whose labors are complete. I moved out to explore the village. The

United church, well screened from the road by a high hedge, was unlocked. It was the standard, simple box architecture but, inside, the stained-glass windows glowed with mellow beauty. In the dim light a ceiling fan softly folded the warm heavy air. I said a stumbling prayer of thanks for the journey so far and for Rob's company—I would miss his dependability and easygoing nature—and returned blinking to the street.

If God was in Tantallon that afternoon He must surely have given full heed to my words, for there was nothing going on to distract Him. The village is shrinking, doomed when the railway left and the grain elevator followed. On cloudy days the distant wail of the trains passing by on the toplands to the north is reflected down into the valley. For the village it is a mournful reminder of better times.

When I entered the town cafe (the building was for sale) I was recognized by several locals. They remembered both my previous visits: once with a dog and once with a girlfriend. The question was inevitable: canoe, girlfriend, dog—which is the best travelling companion? Travel with each has its merits, I answered carefully, but it is perhaps best not to do all at once.

Everyone in town was friendly. In many places in the world society has long ago hardened into a cultural framework closed to outsiders. But people remain rare and valuable commodities on the prairies, and in a prairie town you need do little more than show honest goodwill to be accepted by the locals. Even lifelong prairie inhabitants still feel a bit new and vulnerable, not quite settled in this mysterious land. They value companionship under the great open sky.

There was much talk of bear. There are, indeed, enough of them in the valley around Tantallon to cause problems. The lead-off story concerned a large bear that had killed calves and a colt in one of the coulees, but the details were disputed both in time (the colt was killed years ago) and in fact (the presumed calf corpses were never produced and farmers like to blame predators for lost stock). Secondary ursine case histories followed and grew in the telling. Gradually a construct formed in my mind not of individual incidents and individual bears but rather of a single, idealized Superbear. Bears fascinate because they so resemble people; like us they are adaptable, unpredictable, omnivorous, and fond of processed foods. But bears are indisputably tougher animals than we are. A friend in the bush-and-prairie country north of the valley once crashed at over sixty miles per hour straight into a three-hundred-pound bear; the impact destroyed his station wagon. The bear, although it died later, got up off the highway and shuffled two hundred yards into the bush. By comparison, your own imagination can illustrate what a three-hundred-pound human looks like when hit by a vehicle at highway speed.

More mundane than bear stories, but also pertinent, was advice about the river. There was local consensus that ahead of me lay rich canoeing country free of serious obstacles. I was told that I was lucky the water was high, for at times of low water beavers built dams across the river. We had indeed crossed suspiciously regular rapids earlier, and it was plausible that hidden dams lay underneath. In their journals the traders complained of such dams, since they were damaging to their thin-skinned canoes, but I was happy that beaver were common again in the river. In the tributary coulees of the Qu'Appelle beaver are especially valuable, for their drought-resistant ponds support stable plant communities and benefit a variety of wildlife. In pre-European days beaver ponds were important watering holes for the big game that was the preferred quarry of Plains Indian hunters. Some anthropologists argue convincingly that the Plains Indians fully appreciated the role of the beaver in stabilizing water systems and so were reluctant to hunt beaver for the fur trade, much to the annoyance of the traders, who complained in this regard of Indian "superstitions."

Rob departed late in the afternoon. That night, half-dozing in my tent, I pondered sleepily that you are never so alone as when newly so. The luxury of solitary reflection was short-lived. By midnight, at the latest, it became clear that the campground was also the Friday night stomping ground for the youth of Tantallon. Regrettably, there was more life in the village than I had imagined. Vehicles roared over the open grass, headlights glared, voices laughed and shouted. In the binge style characteristic of all the world's cold-climate countries, much alcohol was being consumed: "partying" it was called when I was younger and is still so called today. To think I could have slept at peace a mile away on some empty hillslope! But insofar as they did not actually drive over the tent, the rowdies were polite; their disturbance was incidental and without malice. As I packed in the predawn gloom the revellers were still up, stoking a bonfire, but now audibly tired. When I hiked off to the canoe it was as if creatures from entirely different worlds were passing each other by, sharing nothing but chance physical proximity; I was almost surprised to understand the language of the strangers' conversation, so disparate our views of life.

Sunrise and moonset were simultaneous this morning. Beautifully illuminated by the sun opposite, in elegant celestial symmetry the full moon floated on the western horizon in the early morning mist. Oh silver moon, you pale and wandering star, what place have we left you in our over-ordered lives? Once you were a mystery and magic to behold; now men have trod upon and scraped your skin, and pronounced you dead, an airless, empty rock. More mystery now in ever-changing prairie grass and prairie water than in your silent, frozen face.

Scanning the shimmering river surface, I saw a stream of bubbles flowing ahead from bank to bank, tracing out the path of swiftest current. Motionless, a doe watched me from the starboard bank, then panicked at my scent when I was well past. In front of the canoe a patch of turf crossed the river as if driven by its own vegetable volition and rootstock, but then I recognized the driver as a muskrat tail. I surprised a raccoon at his morning ablutions on a silt flat; he stared, then sedately moved off into the bush. His calm retreat was a bluff, for it turned to crashing panic when he heard the canoe ground on the flat behind him. I examined his tracks and then pondered the many others; waders aplenty, heron, deer, and animals that I could not identify had all visited in search of water or food. A snake had inscribed an unmistakable signature of miniature barchan dunes, the little crescents facing first one way and then the other.

Initially the course hugged the south-slope hills and so was a woodland paddle, green and pretty, a kingdom of shadow play. As the current quickened and the meanders sharpened, I needed a keen eye and quick reactions to avoid the trees leaning out into the river from the cut banks. Sometimes even in midchannel a tree, still rooted and green, threatened collision. The bouncing waters washed away all thoughts beyond the immediate demands of control and technique. Then the river slowed, left the shelter of the slope woods, and swung north into the rising heat of the open valley bottomlands. The weather was fine, a mix of sun and cloud, and to stay cool I slipped overboard to drift with the canoe. Refreshed and reseated in the canoe, I looked down into the water and saw the overhanging world transmuted through an ever-changing flow of magical distortion. The Qu'Appelle was far superior to a mirror, for to its quaking reflections of sun and cloud and willow above it added its own images of minnows and fish and weed below, feeding the mind more sustenance than mere honest reflection. The solar heat that the river turned back in my inquiring face was clearly real, but a great part of the shapes, colors, and motion that I thought I could see in the depths was illusion. What kind of marvelous watery religion might have developed if Canada had been left to the canoe, the Indians, and the voyageurs for a thousand years? Truly, the gods were rich and multiple on the river.

In midafternoon I pitched camp in the corner of a hayfield. I carefully aligned the tent parallel to the wind. Luckily the breeze was strong enough to discourage mosquitoes. Crows circled above the tent, curious at my intrusion. I could hear rushing water, for at the edge of the hay flat the river had broken through the neck of an old meander. Water plunged through the breach, but the cut was still young and narrow, and much of the river still had to take the original, longer, meander route. In a year or two erosion would widen the breach and the meander would be abandoned completely; its ends would silt up and it would age quietly, growing more marshy and stagnant with each passing year. But perhaps for this year alone it was the perfect route for a swim.

Grasping the tree roots exposed in the banks of the cut, I levered myself twenty metres or so against the current to reach and enter the upstream end of the meander. Then I floated, gently pushed by the current, on a three-hundred-metre journey that returned me to my tent and the cut's churning outflow. Twice more I repeated this satisfying circular journey, stopping en route to examine the many northern leopard frogs plopping in the water around me. Their pale green bodies were tastefully mottled by blotches of darker green; the spotted skin pattern that resulted was the origin of their "leopard" name. But the epithet could as easily have derived from the clean white lines that ran from their eyes back down the length of their bodies, giving them a sleek racing-frog look, like a slick highlighter option on a new sports car. Each time I went round the meander the crows followed me from above in black spirals of silence, as if waiting for something to happen, until finally I became uneasy, wondering if they knew something that I did not.

Resting outside my tent, I listened carefully to the valley, but aside from the rush of wind and water all was silent. Light and shadow flickered in the leaves of the river willows and the wind carried a hint of sage. I had readjusted to solo travel in the natural world; my senses, hungry for landscape detail, were growing more acute. But I was tired, too, and so lay down to read, soon drifting asleep on the riverbank with the blades and early seed-heads of prairie grasses dancing above my head.

When I awoke in the evening both mind and body felt fresh and willing. The dusk had come quickly, like spring comes to the prairie, and caught me unawares. I slipped into the canoe and pushed off, heading upstream. So long as I paddled alongside the hillslopes I was warm, for they radiated the day's retained heat, but out on the open valley floor it was cooler. It was the reverse of the daytime heat pattern. When I crossed the mouth of some unseen coulee a river of cold, heavy air flowed over me as it spilled down onto the valley floor in search of entropy for the night. By contrast the water on my hand was warm and alive. Colours drained away as the light dimmed, leaving a simplified world of greys and blacks where shadow and shape became all-important. The river by night is another world: your hearing sharpens to the point of exaggeration; the senses of smell and touch awaken; and even the tongue slides forward to taste the humid air. The darkness leans ever closer from black-shouldered banks, till the splash of a frog shoots sparks up the spine. On this unknown Qu'Appelle all things but me seemed at ease in the darkness, as if they had known nothing else. From dim river shallows a heron sprang up; its dagger bill and long trailing legs sketched an eerie outline. Beaver and muskrat crisscrossed the river and paid me no heed. Two raccoons scrabbled on the far bank; they too seemed undisturbed by my presence. I turned the canoe back downstream and let it drift while I searched the now soot-black night with all my senses. Hearing the soft creak of bent-back twigs, I scanned with a flashlight. Deer eyes glowed back at me, phosphorescent green, startlingly evil-looking. Starlight flickered in the water while the land around lay heavy and unwelcoming under a cloak of vegetation and thick darkness. I was happy to recognize my little landing beach and return to my tent.

Lying down beside the tent, I fought off returning drowsiness and stared into the night sky. Above me distant suns danced their ponderous ancient waltz. The Great Bear was in the northwest corner of his yearly march around the pole star, the Herdsman was bright in the west, and the Northern Crown floated beside him. The summer stars of the Swan and the Lyre were high above me, the Eagle a little lower down. Not far east from Altair, the white-hot jewel of the Eagle, I found the little Dolphin frozen in arcing flight. The bright stars scattered above me carry Arabic names, exotic to the English ear, a heritage of the clear desert skies of northern Africa and of the Arab science that blossomed during the dark times in Europe after the fall of Rome. The collectives, the constellations, had names long before individual stars. The configurations I knew were Mesopotamian, charted out some six or seven thousand years ago and passed on, via the Phoenicians, to the Greeks. That is why the lion and bear of the Middle East are immortalized in the heavens, but not the elephant of India or Africa. As the constellations are wholly arbitrary, you are welcome to learn those of the Maya or Chinese or, better still, to create your own. Myself, I found buffalo on the horizon that night, safe from the hungry wolf across the sky, and for the first time I saw deer. In my last waking moments I took the antireductionist path and strove to let the symphonic light of two thousand stars play in my head as a great sky-dome collective. In our towns and cities, streetlights flare away our fear of darkness in a blaze of sodium and mercury. Drunk with wealth and noise, we forget God's gift of silent stars—yet who at end of life could defend this disregard before the Lord of Earth and Heaven?

The next morning I was on the water well before sunrise, stroking strongly away from shore to evade a trail of mosquitoes. In the early chill the river steamed like a hot spring. A large owl flew silently through the rising mist, feathers a mottled grey in the shadow-light. When the sun rose it was bright in a clear sky, with a promise of troublesome heat to come. Swinging around a meander, I surprised two raccoons, who were blinded by the sun. They squinted desperately at me as I drifted to within three metres before they waddled awkwardly over the bank.

Ducks were again numerous. One dysfunctional teal was almost tiresome in her foolishness. After quacking far behind me, safe with her brood, she made a belated decision to panic. Leaving her ducklings, she flew up ahead of the canoe to perform a particularly bad broken wing act. She then lifted off, but rather than return to her young, repeated her performance two hundred metres farther on, only desisting in order to fly ahead for yet a third act in this unnecessary drama.

Sadder was the case of the young Canada geese I caught up to on a straight reach. Refusing to head into the banks and unable to fly, they were also unwilling to let me pass by on the side. No matter what ruse I tried, they swam on ahead of me, for something over a kilometre. Finally, where the river widened, I managed to sneak by all but one goose. Isolation magnified his fear and he dove underwater ahead of me. Seizing the chance, I paddled hard to get past him while he was still submerged. Unhappily, he swam forward too and suddenly popped up, exhausted, directly beside the canoe. Terrified, he dove again, only to emerge a mere two metres ahead, almost drowned. As I slid past his enfeebled body he gasped for breath with pitiable croaks. He was not so much afraid now as resigned to a death-blow from this huge predator-canoe. I watched him behind me until after several minutes he recovered and moved toward shore.

Not much farther on, under a warm sun, was true death: massive, half-rotted, covered in flies and seething with maggots. The smell was foul and I had to paddle carefully to remain upwind of the whitetail buck carcass sprawled half-immersed in the river. Though the hindquarters had been chewed out, there were no animal tracks in the surrounding mud. I remembered the fence post vulture, that earlier, unsubtle message about the natural balance of the river. Dutch biologist Midas Dekkers, who argues that decay is life and life is decay, revels in carrion, and would have been as delighted as any vulture with my find. Dekkers abhors our obsession with the preservation and conservation of artifacts and organisms and would do away with museums—how much more natural, he believes, to just watch things fall apart and let wild nature run its rampant course. It is an intriguing philosophy from a man who, not surprisingly, hates the spring, the season of organized renewal. But when I studied the carcass I saw that this particular death had not been easy; the buck's eyes stared opaque, but clearly terrified. I paddled away subdued.

At exactly 10:10 A.M. (11:10 A.M. for Manitobans) I reached the Manitoba-Saskatchewan boundary. There was no cairn or signage, but the boundary was clearly indicated by a cable used to guide a raft across the river. The raft, roughly constructed out of oil drums and sheet plywood, was a platform for the water flow measurements needed to ensure fair apportionment of scarce prairie water between the provinces. I beached to explore on the starboard bank. The river ahead curled back on itself hard to starboard, so I was standing on a small point. It was clothed in tall grass and had a pretty bluff of Manitoba maple at its end. A nervous plover followed my reconnaissance from above, complaining loudly. In the strong wind it was much cooler on land than on the water. On the north valley slope I saw the long, angled scar of the Canadian National mainline climbing out of the valley. Train echoes were frequent here. Immediately across the river were hay bales and abandoned farm equipment left to rust overlooking the river.

I relaunched. There were light rapids, but it was easy to duck underneath the cable as the canoe passed into Manitoba. This being the Qu'Appelle, at 10:28 A.M. the river swung me back into Saskatchewan, as if to allow a moment for reflection and nostalgia, and then at 10:30 A.M. we meandered definitively into the Keystone Province.

Most of the river's windings were now in the centre of the valley, where I was fully exposed to sun and wind. The increasing bottomlands heat ground me down as the day progressed. Three hours into Manitoba I beached and crawled out of the canoe, dehydrated and badly in need of shade and shelter. The river was almost stagnant and so heavy with mud that it looked like I should be able to pick it up and shape it like Plasticine; even I, not the most discriminating swimmer, would not swim in this swampy brew. At least the trees near my landing site here at the foot of the north-slope hills offered welcome shade. I pitched tent and crawled in, thinking only of rest and cold, clean water.

For a long time I sprawled semiconscious, brain and body cooling. Not until evening was I rested enough to wander up to the top of the slope hills. I climbed deliberately, my river legs complaining at the unaccustomed uphill work. As I crested the valley I stopped and stared, astonished at the vast landscape that confronted me. Pushed aside by my experiences of river life in the valley below, my memories of the great flatlands above had dimmed. Yet the prairie had been with me always. Before me a great plain stretched away forever in overwhelming silence. Immediately ahead of me was a barley field and beyond it, visible in binoculars, was a turning wind pump, soundless at this distance. I walked west along the valley edge and into an empty pasture. Perched on a fence wire, a sparrow swallowed a grasshopper then neatly cleaned its beak on a barb. Heifers in the adjacent field farther west moved off nervously when they saw me, kicking up a cloud of dust that hung bloody orange against the setting sun. Their hooves thudded dully on arid earth, the sound almost lost in the vastness. They stopped and stared back at me, black silhouettes seen through a warm-toned haze. Silence flooded back to the plain. Now that my journey was coming to an end I felt less hostile toward the cattle, fellow creatures in this empty land. Despite the rising dust their pasture appeared not to be overgrazed. It was only that the soil was very light and dry.

To the north, directly away from the valley edge, was a slight rise, an eminence, as the old prairie travellers would have called it, perhaps not even two metres higher than the surrounding flatlands. It was natural that I should search out an anchor in this landscape devoid of references, and I struck out toward the rise in a dead straight line. It was hard to judge the distance, but in twenty minutes I had reached my objective and won a slightly raised view. Standing elevated, alone on the Plains, the space was staggering, at once terrifying and exhilarating; it reminded me of a roller-coaster ride as a child. Indeed I felt young, fully alive, rejuvenated by pure space, like an ember fired by oxygen. With my senses spinning, wholeness and harmony rose up inside me; I was overcome by a euphoria of belonging. *This land is of me, and I am of this land*—it was a certainty in my belly. Yet it was a certainty tight-bound in incomprehension, for it was impossible to ever understand this land; its scale was inhuman. The prairies were like a beloved spouse: simultaneously alien and part of your heart. I felt sudden understanding for those who pass through the prairies quickly on four wheels, cocooned in steel and glass. After a few more uncomprehending minutes atop my prairie summit, adrift in the prairie, I turned and walked back to the valley, puzzled, humbled, euphoria fading. As I reached the slopes and began my descent the two kilometre wide valley seemed a small and cozy place compared to the unintelligible vastness above. Night was falling and coyotes above and behind me broke the grassland silence to weave their own understanding of the prairies.

Much later, lying drowsy in my tent, I listened to the train whistles: deep, visceral wails, pushing far out into the prairie night. In Britain the train whistles are high-pitched shrieks, their shrillness well suited to cutting through the cacophonous clamor of a crowded industrial land. The empty prairies provide no such aural competition and so the pitch is set low and far-reaching, alerting prairie dwellers many miles distant to the rumbling passage of smoke, diesel, and iron.

In the morning I rose late and was not on the water until well after sunrise, for it was now not far to St. Lazare and the Assiniboine River. On the north valley slopes I saw an eastbound passenger train descending into the valley, a rare sight in these modern times when so few people travel the prairies by rail. Soon there was a cultural clue on the starboard bank that a town lay not far ahead: miscellaneous garbage and a pile of wrecked cars overlooking the river. Then came a natural clue to the nearness of river's end: *Phragmites australis*, common reed-grass, in the middle of the channel, indicating the absence of current.

I slowed now, melancholy threatening at the thought my journey was ending. The river had given me a clear sense of direction, place, and purpose. What could be more natural than to paddle downstream in a canoe? I was saddened that the Qu'Appelle was stagnant and tired, heavy with sediment, all youthful energy gone. It had aged quicker than I.

At the river junction the current of the Assiniboine kicked hard at the stern of a lazy Qu'Appelle canoe. I strained to straighten my craft and then turned it upstream for a reconnaissance of the unknown Assiniboine. It was only slightly wider than the Qu'Appelle, but there was more energy in the Assiniboine here than it showed far downstream in Winnipeg. After paddling a short reach I turned back and returned to the confluence of the sister rivers. The point of land that marked this union was solid bush, inaccessible by land. Undistinguished in every way, it was as mundane a marriage of rivers as can be imagined. The united waters flowed on in a river course widened to the simple sum of the width of the two rivers upstream of the forks. This gave the impression that the Qu'Appelle and the Assiniboine travelled together purely as a matter of convenience, but both rivers were equally murky, so it was difficult to see how quickly the two commingled below their union.

Four or five kilometres downstream from the forks is the site of Fort Ellice. It was to here that stubborn Archibald McDonald struggled from Fort Qu'Appelle for six miserable weeks with his poplar-plank boats. Until the arrival of the railway Fort Ellice was the Hudson's Bay Company entrepôt for the Qu'Appelle and Upper Assiniboine watersheds. The site, elevated on a plateau above the river, is barren now, marked only by a commemorative cairn. The cairn is technically not accessible by land, for the only road access is blocked by a large "No Trespassing" sign. It saddened me to see access to a nation's heritage denied.

From the forks I paddled back up the Qu'Appelle a few hundred metres, made landfall, and walked into town along railway and road. A large highway sign, "We mourn 25 years of abortion," confronts visitors and residents. In the infinite space of the prairies, abortion is hard to understand. The village's most attractive building was an old convent. It was in good shape, with a fine cupola, and the order's name, *Présentation de Marie*, tastefully inscribed on the façade.

Among the townsfolk I encountered little knowledge of, or interest in, the

Qu'Appelle. Ignorance of upstream and downstream geography would have been unimaginable in earlier days. But freight now runs on roads, and the daily paper arrives from distant Winnipeg, while almost all of the Qu'Appelle Valley lies on the far side of a political boundary that is more relevant for residents than is the lay of the land.

St. Lazare is very French and very Catholic. As elsewhere in the world, culture, language, and religion interlock and reinforce each other. The village church is a modern structure set on a small rise a block off main street, but, unlike most recent Catholic churches, it was not built to the squarish floor plan that the Roman Catholic Church has adapted from English nonconformist architecture. Where the nonconformists sought to centre the congregation around the pulpit, the modern Catholic Church wishes to mass parishioners around the altar. The isolated parishioners of St. Lazare have rejected this idea in favour of the traditional long nave. The roof is high and steeply pitched, and its great length amplifies the moans of the wind outside. Judging by the building's generous dimensions, the congregation must be large for the village's size. Pro-life newspapers were prominent in the entrance hall. On the sanctuary wall, beside the cross and the risen Christ, was a silhouette of a traditional family captioned in an arc: "*Gardez la famille en vie.*" The father, slightly larger than the mother, had the oldest child, a boy, on his left; the mother, with a traditional dress and long hair, held the hand of the younger daughter on her right. It was that favourite ensemble used in commercial advertising: marketing research has revealed that the North American family ideal is two parents and two children and, more precisely, that the elder child should be a boy of eleven and the younger a girl of nine. But there was a third child here too, a little girl, at the hand of her older sister. The message was clear: there is always room for one more in the family of God.

Tiring of buildings and urban structure, I climbed up the east side of the Assiniboine Valley, making for a large cross erected atop the valley's edge. It was an echo of the similar but still larger cross that overlooked Lebret in the Qu'Appelle Valley far to the west. The St. Lazare cross was electrified and the power cable ran half-buried down the slope, but the bulbs had been removed. Not far away on the toplands was the village cemetery and within it a toolshed disguised as a tiny chapel. With steel siding and a padlocked door, the shed looked incongruous rather than pious.

Unlike their European ancestors, many prairie townsfolk bury their dead away from the townsite. In consequence most prairie graveyards are solitary places. As you wander through them the stubborn verticality of the living is accentuated by the horizontal repose of the dead, who rest congruent with the spirit of the Plains. At St. Lazare the dead crowd close to valley's edge. The effect is striking, and must be intentional, for the visitor's sake, if not for those entombed. Below, the Assiniboine Valley spreads wide with canola and hay flats. Across and beyond the valley, the solemn land flows on forever. The vast scale of the view from valley's edge makes any other emotion but loneliness improbable, quite apart from the sad whisper of the grass in the ever-present prairie wind and the thought of the stretched-out bones of those sheltered below in quiet soil. Lazare—Lazarus in English—he who rose from the dead. Was such a triumph over nature not a vain hope here on the all-levelling Plains?

In his "Testament" of 1845 poet Taras Schevchenko entreated that he be buried after death on the western shore of the Steppes' seas of grass in a great grave mound high above the Dnieper. The placid Assiniboine winding below had not the roar of the Dnieper rapids, where the commerce of the open Steppes once crossed over into the settled farmlands of Europe, yet from this dramatic graveyard viewpoint I understood the poet's yearning. Most poignant, in these prairie lands where all memory seems doomed to be sucked dry and blown away by the tireless wind, was his final request: "With softly spoken, kindly word, pray, men, remember me."

Forcing melancholy aside, I looked west, and could see for kilometres up the Qu'Appelle, perhaps into Saskatchewan. The Qu'Appelle Valley slopes were bushy and wooded here at their eastern limits, as if the prairie itself was dying away. My eyes drifted restlessly up and down the valley of the calling Spirit, for I felt drawn to return. Like the valley itself, my river journey had ended.

CHAPTER SIX

HORSE

HORSES AND THE PRAIRIES fit each other like hand and glove. It is hard to believe that horses were as foreign to the New World as the Europeans who brought them here. In truth, the sixteenth-century Spanish only reintroduced an earlier reality, for the ancestors of the modern horse, protohorses of the genus *Equus*, first evolved in North America. From here they crossed the Bering Strait land bridge and colonized the Old World, while dying out in their Western Hemisphere homeland. One explanation for the horse's North American demise links the disappearance of a number of native megafauna like mastodon, mammoth, camel, and horse to the roughly simultaneous arrival of man in the New World some fourteen thousand years ago. Large North American mammals, according to this theory, had not co-evolved with human hunters and lacked effective defence strategies against the enterprising new predators from Asia. The explosively expanding front of human invaders, set loose in a hunter's virgin paradise, swept the great American mammals into extinction.

It is a spectacular hypothesis with confusing implications. On the one hand it implies that Stone Age man was more efficient, well organized, and generally "advanced" than most people recognize. Yet the theory also links an aboriginal population with major ecological disruption. Many liberal-minded people like to view aboriginal peoples as socially responsible ecological managers living according to nonmaterialistic precepts. It is, after all, in terms of its hypermaterialism and ecological indifference that the industrial world appears to fail, and it is some consolation to believe that other peoples hold the secret to a sustainable lifestyle. How depressing it is to think that, except by the accident of technological limitations, perhaps no people lives, or has ever lived, in respectful balance with nature.

Whatever the explanation for its ancestors' disappearance, the reintroduced modern horse thrived on the New World grasslands. Many old Pleistocene enemies, like the sabre-toothed tiger, were now extinct, and the wide-open sight lines made it easy to spot those predators, like the wolf, that remained. Horses can have footing problems in mountainous country, or in exposed soft soils, whether sandy or wet, but the prairie blanket of grass was ideal, supplying cushioned traction as well as food to beyond the horizon.

The spectacular success of the horse on the Pampas predates the history of the horse on the Plains. In 1536 the Spanish mounted what was for the time a huge expedition to the Pampas coast, sixteen ships and sixteen hundred men, and founded a fort at the site of modern Buenos Aires. At this early point in New World colonial history the Spanish were driven almost exclusively by a hunger for gold and silver. There were two necessary conditions for Spanish success: first, a source of precious metal and, second, a settled indigenous agricultural population that could be subjugated and parasitized for food and labour. Despite their initial optimism (Buenos Aires is sited near the mouth of the river they named, in vain, *Río de la Plata*, "River of Silver"), the Spanish found that neither of these conditions held on the Pampas. Most troublesomely, the local indigenous population, the Querandí, were nomadic hunters, not settled farmers. There was no agricultural surplus for the Spanish to appropriate, and the mobility of the Querandí made them impossible to control.

The Spanish had previously seized what became Mexico City with five hundred men and mastered the Inca empire with a force of two hundred, so it was a tremendous shock for them to suffer military defeat against the foot-bound Querandí. The Spanish fortifications were vulnerable to burning by the

Querandí's flaming arrows and the Spaniards' awe-inspiring new weapon, the horse, fell crashing to the *bolas.* With this simple weapon of leather and sewn-in rocks whipped and released from overhead, the Querandí were adept at bringing down the little Pampas deer with the same skill with which Pampas cowboys would later lasso cattle. In comparison to deer the large legs of Spanish warhorses were an easy target. Within a year guerrilla warfare had reduced the Spanish to starvation in their fort. The expedition's German chronicler, Ulrich Schmidt, wrote of their plight:

> Yea, finally, there was such want and misery for hunger's sake, that there were neither rats, nor mice, nor snakes to still the dreadful hunger and unspeakable poverty, and shoes and leather were resorted to for eating and everything else. It happened that three Spaniards stole a horse and ate it secretly, but when it was known, they were imprisoned and interrogated under the torture. Whereupon, as soon as they admitted their guilt, they were sentenced to death by the gallows, and all three were hanged. Immediately afterwards, at night, three other Spaniards came to the gallows to the three hanging men, and hacked off their thighs and pieces of their flesh, and took them home to still their hunger. A Spaniard also ate his brother, who died in the city of Buenos Aires.

No wonder, then, that the Spanish entirely abandoned the Pampas coast in search of better fortune elsewhere. But they left a legacy behind. The few horses and cattle that had escaped the fort multiplied rapidly in the rich grassland. When after many years the Spanish returned to the Pampas, they found a world transformed, where untold millions of horses and cattle roamed wild. The Native American was now mounted and provided renewed and effective resistance to the slow Spanish colonization of the Pampas. The horse had come into its own and remains, like its modern master, the gaucho, a central part of Pampas culture.

In North America the Spanish introduced horses to Mexico and from there took them north into what is now the American Southwest, in particular to the stock-raising area around Santa Fe, thought to be the original source of Plains horses. No one knows precisely how the first southern Plains tribes acquired the horse, but familiarization with the animal was inevitable, given simple powers of observation and the fact that the Spanish found it necessary to train at least some indigenous peoples in horse management to help look after European cattle. The spread of the horse northward across the Plains, whether by war, theft, escape, or trade, began around 1630. Horses finally reached what are now the Canadian prairies in the 1730s, although they did not become common there until several decades later still. For the Indians the new beast of burden (called "big dog" in some Native languages) was a great boon. The dog travois was reconfigured and enlarged to fit the horse and loaded with goods over a hundred kilograms in weight during seasonal migrations. Extra food, skins and clothing, large quantities of buffalo hides, the pots and pans acquired from the traders, and the heavy lodgepoles used to construct spectacular tepees, all could be carried or pulled by horses; no longer was material culture restricted to that which could be moved by dogs or people.

As important as its superior ability to move goods was the fact that the horse magnified the range and power of the traveller, the hunter, and the warrior. A wealthy individual would own a string of horses and employ different mounts to different ends. For travois use an older, experienced saddle horse was favoured, for it was less likely to panic when constrained by the dragging shafts. The most valuable animal was the best hunting or warhorse, which had to be brave, fast, and responsive. Tack varied to suit the purpose: strong wood and horn saddles were used on the travois horses and light pad saddles were employed for the hunt or battle. Contrary to Hollywood myth, Indians did not customarily ride bareback.

While they often regretted the many other consequences of contact with Europeans, Native peoples always expressed gratitude for the "Great Gift" of the horse—indeed, one Plains vision of paradise imagined (or imagines still?) the gift of the horse followed by the tactful disappearance of the white man. For their part the white traders viewed the horse with mixed feelings, since it contributed to Indian power and self-sufficiency. The horse also gave the chief traders' hired men undesirable independence. The men could, for example, choose to take with them all the distractions of family life when they travelled on business. In 1803 a grumpy Alexander Henry observed: "It is true they are useful animals, but if there were not one [horse] in all the North West, we should have less trouble and expense. Our men would neither be so burdened with families, nor so indolent and insolent as they are, and the natives in general would be more honest and industrious. Let an impartial eye look into the affair, to discover whence originates the unbounded extravagance of our meadow gentry, both white and native, and horses will be found one of the principal causes."

Life for the horses themselves was tough. In 1800 Henry reported on the horses he saw in the Manitoba prairies: "The poor brutes are in a shocking condition; some of them, as soon as they are unsaddled, will bite and tear the raw flesh until the blood flows, and then kick and roll for some time, whilst their whole bodies quiver and they appear to be in agony. Indians and Canadians ride horses in this condition with the greatest composure, and no care is taken of them." Ideally a rider would take several horses on a raid, hunting trip, or long journey, for the mounts would tire and were best used in rotation. But if necessary any Plainsman, Henry included, would ride a horse into the ground.

Plains Indian horses are more properly called ponies, for they averaged about thirteen and a half hands high at the withers, five centimetres under official horse size. Traders' journals provide a record of the animals' physique and characteristics. Anthony Hendry, who in 1754 was the first European to describe horses on the northern Plains, was favorably impressed. He wrote that they were "fine tractible animals, about 14 hands high; lively and clean made." Many later observers were less convinced of the pony's aesthetic merits. Horse connoisseur Theodore Dodge stated that the Indian pony "is not handsome. His middle piece is distended by grass food . . . He has a hammer head and . . . pronounced ewe neck." Illustrator Frederic Remington emphasized the pony's practical rather than aesthetic build, noting that "the head and neck join like the two parts of a hammer," and he described the pony's belly as "a veritable tun." Even the mane was shabby to his eye, as likely to fall half to each side as cleanly to one shoulder. Cavalryman Richard Dodge, while acknowledging that the ponies had not the slightest appearance of "blood," was more complimentary. The Indian pony, he wrote, "is rather slight in build, although always having powerful forequarters, good legs, short strong back, and full barrel."

The lifestyle the Plains horse peoples developed is unique in world history. To a degree they became pastoralists, for as horse owners they had to consider problems of shelter, forage, and water for their stock. On the cold northern Plains, horses, unlike the buffalo, could not paw their way through the snow to the frozen grass, so supplemental winter feeding was sometimes necessary. The Blackfoot, for example, stripped the bark off cottonwood trees for winter feed. However, unlike the true pastoralists of the Old World, the Plains Indians had no cattle, sheep, or goats and instead still depended on the hunt for food. Compared to pastoralists, hunters live in smaller groups, have a looser social structure, and, unrestricted by livestock, are faster and more flexible in their movements. These distinctions provide insight into the differing histories of the mounted Plains Indians and their cousins in lifestyle, the pastoralist Steppe peoples.

In contrast to the Plains Indians, the Steppe peoples needed to organize and execute grazing migrations, driven by the seasons or by drought, with military precision. Pacts between nomadic Steppe peoples were essential to planning migration routes and maintaining grazing rights. Driven by circumstance to build elaborate alliances and to become expert field strategists, it was only natural that the talent, courage, and charisma of the occasional outstanding leader—an Attila, a Tamerlane, or a Ghengis—could forge a union of Steppe peoples strong enough to exploit the full potential of the horse and unleash a campaign of imperial conquest.

Writing of the Scythians in the fifth century B.C., the Greek historian Herodotus provides the earliest written records of European contact with

Steppe peoples. Lacking settlements and agriculture, the Scythians were, like the Pampas Querandí, unconquerable, and to pursue them was as futile as to chase the Steppe winds:

> The Scythian nation has made the most clever discovery among all the people we know, and of the one thing that is greatest in human affairs—though for the rest I do not admire them much. This greatest thing . . . is how no invader who comes against them can ever escape and none can catch them if they do not wish to be caught. For this people has no cities or settled forts; they carry their houses with them and shoot with bows from horseback; they live off herds of cattle, not from tillage, and their dwellings are on their wagons. How then can they fail to be invincible and inaccessible for others?

Originally the Steppe nomads were merely annoyingly proud and independent neighbors to the populous agricultural civilizations of China, India, and Mesopotamia. But the invention of the stirrup around the second century B.C. somewhere on the Asian Steppes enabled the rider to have much greater control in battle over horse and weapons. Refinement of the logistics of equestrian pastoralism, together with the stirrup and other advances in the arts of cavalry war, made the Steppe nations not just invulnerable to attack but also powerful aggressors who regularly overran and parasitized neighboring agricultural heartlands. Only the sea or impenetrable forest put a natural limit to the ambitions of the Steppe cavalries. Of all Steppe nations the Mongols are the most famous, but they were only one people among many who, despite attempts at defence as astonishing as the Great Wall of China, were a threat to settled peoples from the Pacific to Europe even into the 1800s.

Centuries sometimes separated the waves of attacking horsemen, but the aggressors always had in common a contempt for farming peoples that is echoed today in the sometimes condescending attitude of the rancher toward his farming cousin. Historian Charles Fitzgerald notes that when the Mongols invaded

China they were disgusted to find the entire country cultivated. How, they wondered, could people who supported themselves "on top of a weed" expect respect? Genghis Khan, among many claims to fame, ranks as an eco-visionary of the first order, for he came close to enacting an extraordinary conservation plan. After the conquest of the great grasslands of northern China that followed his capture of Beijing in 1215, he intended to put to death the entire hundred-million-strong crop-farming peasantry in order to allow the land to revert to natural grass. Such reclaimed pasture would have been well suited to the needs of the Mongols, their beloved horses, and their stock animals. The great Khan, a grassland purist, was only dissuaded from what seemed to him the obvious thing to do by the lure of great riches, for the Mongols could exact a steady flow of tribute from a living, subjugated, Chinese peasantry. So, like many after him, Genghis abandoned his environmental ideals for material gain.

The foot-bound Plains Indians had been few in number compared to their agricultural neighbors to the east and south or to the rich hunter-gatherers of the Pacific coast. But the horse made life on the prairie a much more promising proposition. At the same time as the horse became widespread on the Plains many Native peoples were under direct or indirect pressure from European settlement and expansion inland from the Atlantic coast. European pressure and the attraction of the horse together brought some eastern woodland nations out onto the Plains. Even for some peoples not under pressure the lure of the horse and prairie was motivation enough. The Comanche, a foot-bound nation of hunter-gatherers living in the southwestern cordillera, expanded eastward onto the Plains purely to take advantage of the new opportunities—and to eventually become a legendary horse people.

Like the pastoralists of Asia, the newly mounted peoples of the Plains were sometimes a threat to neighboring farmers. The Mandans, who grew squash and maize in the bottomlands of the Missouri River Valley, found themselves almost helpless against mounted attack. In response, like some peoples in the boundary zone between the Plains and the eastern woodlands, they began to shift from agriculture to a hunter-gatherer lifestyle, themselves taking advantage of the horse to hunt the buffalo. According to classical thought, which sees as natural the progression from hunter-gathering to agriculture to industrialized civilization, this is a dubious reversal of human destiny. The classical view derives from our odd assumption that "progress" is definable, linear, and inevitable, a culturally prejudiced belief no older than the Enlightenment. Surely the life of the buffalo hunter is as good as that of the factory employee!

What might have been the ultimate ends of Plains history if the dream of the horse without the white man had been reality? It is conceivable that buffalo numbers might have come under pressure as more and more Native peoples took to the horse and the buffalo hunt. Another megafauna extinction would not have been impossible. If a human population crash followed, the horse would have been the agent of only a burst of prosperity, a glorious false dawn. Yet in the absence of the buffalo the horse itself could have become the dominant food staple. And it is in any case perfectly imaginable that a sustainable horse-buffalo balance might have been struck.

One advantage of horses was that they could transport a much greater kill weight than dogs, so there was potential for greater usage of buffalo meat, bone, and fiber. Most importantly, the horse allowed Indian hunters to be selective about the type and number of buffalo killed, for the mounted hunter could ride into a buffalo herd and pick out individual animals. In the Dog Age, by contrast, hunters had to depend on mass kills. One mass hunt technique depended for success on the notoriously poor eyesight of buffalo. An agile hunter disguised in a buffalo robe would decoy a herd to a cliff edge and then leap over the brink to safety on a hidden ledge, while overhead the buffalo plunged to their deaths. A herd of buffalo could also be prodded forward from behind by hunters in wolf skins. Other hunters, strategically placed along the sides of the desired drive path, kept the herd from turning aside. While the final stampede might be dramatic, the slow driving of the buffalo could take days of careful maneuvering and resembled a cautious herding exercise as much as a hunt. A successful drive might yield hundreds of buffalo, perhaps more than could be effectively used. Equally, if the buffalo turned aside at the last moment, the hunting party could end up without a single animal.

On the Kazakh Steppes saiga antelope were hunted in a similar manner, but instead of using a cliff or impoundment site hunters built an *aran*, a set of two converging fence lines. The converging lines did not quite meet, ending instead in a narrow gap—what a rancher would recognize as "the chute." Stiff cattail stems, bound and cut to a sharp edge, were fitted to the chute posts. When a herd of saiga was chased into the funnel trap, panicked animals in front were forced through the chute by the pressure of those behind. Some saiga squeezed through and survived, some died days later from wounds and infection, and some died quickly, disemboweled by the honed reed blades. But even these latter unfortunates were able to stumble on a few dozen metres before collapsing, which made room for the next victim through the chute. Saiga horns were especially prized in Chinese medicine: a pair of horns was equal to a horse or camel in value. In the nineteenth century the killing of saiga turned industrial, just as it did for buffalo on the prairies. In these later hunts there are records of up to twelve thousand saiga killed in a single day using the *aran*.

If you imagine an alternative Plains history, with the horse and without Europeans, another question arises besides the fate of the buffalo. How would Plains peoples have related to their non-Plains neighbors? Not being true pastoralists, Plains peoples would not have been driven to forge the migratory grazing pacts that on the Steppes were a stepping stone to alliances for foreign conquest. Yet for mobile Plains nations the riches of the Aztecs to the south would have been as great a prize as China was for the Steppe peoples. Perhaps some great grassland conqueror might have risen who was tempted by Aztec gold.

We will never know. The Aztec Empire indeed fell to horsemen, but to Hernán Cortés and his conquistadors, not to Native North Americans. The fate of the buffalo was indeed sealed, but likewise not by the Indian. The white man stayed and he brought far more than horses; he brought killing diseases and then an insatiable hunger for land. The nomadic nature of their life on the Plains gave the Indians some defense against the intruders, just as it had saved the Querandí on the Pampas centuries earlier, but the respite was temporary. Ultimately, by war, treaty, starvation, and disease, the Indian nations were broken.

History was then written by the farmer and the rancher, not by the buffalo peoples. Steel ploughs and foreign seeds split the Plains earth as the farmer turned over the land ("wrong side up," according to the old Native lament) and pushed away buffalo and Indian to remote corners of the prairie and consciousness. There they remain, suffocated by the immigrant pioneer's plough-and-grow ethic. The horse travois disappeared with the buffalo, replaced by carts and wagons, although the horse itself continued to be essential to Native and immigrant alike for decades after agricultural settlement. But ultimately, to all but a few ranchers, the horse too lost its value, supplanted by machines made in factories far away.

DESPITE LOSING its original raisons d'être, the horse has survived the aftermath of white settlement, for although horses now exist largely only as recreational or ceremonial relics, they have never been totally out of favour among the new prairie populace. Nothing looks finer in the town parade than a team of well-trained horses. But, like most modern prairie dwellers, I had little personal experience of horses. If I was to rebuild the old horse travois and renew old travois trails, I had much to learn about riding and managing horses, about horse mind and horse body. A year after my canoe journey I was hanging around stables and other people's mounts, absorbing the odd bits of horsey lore that flow freely from those who know and love this noble animal. From observation I progressed to riding lessons. My instructor was direct, wasting no time on civilities: "There's your horse" did service for "Hello." Not being a "natural" rider, I provided as much amusement as cash. In the early days I was saddle-sore much of the time and sympathized with Alexander Henry's suffering after a particularly rough prairie ride. Near the North Saskatchewan River in November of 1809 he wrote: "Found myself very unwell, with a high fever and sore throat, proceeding,

I believe, from my violent exercise in coming from Moose creek, when I rode the most rough and cruel-going mare I ever straddled. She had neither gallop, canter, nor trot, but all three combined to tear my entrails out, and severely did I feel the effect of her cursed gait."

As my skills improved I graduated to more difficult mounts, though none were as demanding as Henry's. Eager to widen my experience, I also searched for horses outside of lessons. One day I secured permission at a communal farm to try riding a Morgan that had been unridden for the previous eight months. My first mistake was timing, for when I walked the horse into an L-shaped paddock it was noon in the prairie West and the farmhands, eager for dinner-time entertainment, were free to gather to watch horse and stranger. Surrounded by unexpected public interest, I felt like the protagonist in some old-time Western—but I was uncertain of the script. I had judged it wiser to first start off with the unfamiliar horse in the enclosed corral before heading for open country, but I was shaken when I saw the hummocky, stony ground in the paddock and the nails protruding from the post that anchored the inside corner at the elbow of the "L." More worrying still was a shed roof of corrugated sheet steel that projected over the fence and into the corral. It was a floating, serrated knife-edge, above horse height, but at neck height for an unwary rider. Keeping all these dangers in mind, I mounted carefully, trying to appear confident to both horse and farmhands. Although good-tempered, after a winter's long freedom the Morgan was edgy under an unfamiliar rider. The onlookers slapped themselves with laughter and roared their appreciation as I nearly lost control of the horse coming fast around the elbow of the "L." I managed to recover and turn the horse at the last second, just narrowly avoiding a ragged beheading on the corrugated roof. Terrified, but feigning nonchalance, I announced that "the new boy" was ready to take the horse out into open country. This proved a wise move: on fallow I could ride safely, even at a gallop, while my hat, forever flying off my head, made a good marker for manoeuvres and pick-up drills. Alone in these open fields, I tasted the horseman's freedom and power and his easy, natural arrogance.

Having survived basic training in horsemanship, I needed a mount, and preferably one as close in type to the old Plains Indian ponies as possible. Sadly, like the Plains Indian dog, the true Indian ponies have disappeared. Native peoples lost their original stock of horses in the reservation and reserve era; where they still keep horses the animals are usually of similar bloodlines to standard North American stock. I could not expect it to be easy to find an accurate replicate among anyone's modern herd, for farming and sport horses tend, like Morgans, to be bigger than the old Indian ponies, but my research had at least given me a good idea of the physique and temperament that I was looking for.

Just as on my dog search two years earlier, after a few false trails I struck it lucky. Tiny was a thirteen-year-old mare of mixed blood who closely matched the old descriptions of Indian ponies. Standing thirteen and a half hands high, she was sturdy, with straight shoulders and strong legs, a large head, a split mane, and a generous belly that belied her name. She had led an outdoors life throughout the coldest prairie winters and had a healthy, self-reliant disposition. Her temperament was easygoing and she was neither overly friendly nor shy of people. Best of all, she came complete with the advice of a wise and sympathetic owner willing to lend her out for a summer. My travois plans would have as good a chance with her as with any horse.

I rode Tiny daily while turning my attention to horse travois construction. There seemed no better plan of action than to again follow Buffalo-bird-woman's detailed instructions. She specified green ash trees for the main travois shafts, but the required straight, five-metre lengths of standing timber were almost non-existent in the valley. Green ash is not a common valley tree to begin with, and most straight sections of timber have long ago found their way into local fence posts. After hard searching in the valley's tributary coulees, I found a single suitable tree. Days later, after almost despairing, I found a suitable match. A handsaw brought them both down.

A further day's work in the hills sufficed to find the smaller cross pieces needed to build the travois load rack. I set to work debarking and, when that tedious job was complete, moved on to assembly. The great size of the horse travois, spreading over one and a half metres across at the base, made it much more unwieldy than the dog travois, but construction itself was simpler, requiring no skins or stitching, and the horse travois proved quicker to build. When I led Tiny around the completed travois, she was, in the manner of her kind, suspicious of this strange and novel object. A moment of truth was at hand.

Proper horse trainers introduce horses to new tasks slowly and by degree. For a sensible introduction to travois I might have had Tiny first drag a pole behind her on a rope, before progressing to pulling a single pole hitched alongside her saddle, before finally pulling the complete travois. Or I might have affixed progressively heavier weights to a leather hide pulled by ropes hitched to the saddle. In buffalo days Indian boys surfed on hides dragged by ponies as part of breaking them to travois. But I was impatient and, encouraged by the confidence of Tiny's owner, Errol, decided to move directly to full travois training. Errol was keen to assist at the critical moment, partly for his own amusement and partly out of concern for his horse. With Tiny tied to a fence post, we carefully hitched up the two travois shafts either side of her saddle. With her body confined between the shafts running alongside her flanks, Tiny shifted her feet uneasily.

I untied Tiny from the fence and led her cautiously for her first few steps with the travois. Her body swayed from side to side as she shied from contact with the shaft on her left flank, only to encounter the shaft on her right. Slowly I guided her around the paddock. Occasionally she stopped when unhappy with pressure on one of her flanks; occasionally she sped up nervously when the dragging shaft ends grated loudly over stony ground. The travois indeed fit too snugly; obviously in her time Buffalo-bird-woman had dealt with svelter horses. I took a few measurements and we unhitched the travois. I then set to work adjusting travois width, encouraged that things were working out well.

A few days later I was on foot leading Tiny with travois over open pasture. Things had been going very smoothly at walking pace and I had begun to wonder how Tiny would perform with travois at a trot. Without thinking the idea

Travois troubles

through properly, I upped my pace to a slow jog; alongside me Tiny's legs broke smoothly into the elegant cater-corner cadence of the trot. But the trot is a much rougher pace than the walk and the travois bounced behind her, setting the shafts vibrating against her flanks. Unnerved by this, Tiny sped up slightly. I in turn had to jog faster to keep up. Already I knew I had made a terrible mistake. The faster Tiny trotted, the more the travois bounced, and the faster she trotted. Within the space of a few seconds I had to run full tilt to keep up and had lost all control of the situation.

If I could just have gotten in front of Tiny, I could have stopped her. Pulling her head sharply sideways toward me would normally have worked as well, for the body must needs follow the head. But the travois shafts projected well in front of Tiny's shoulders and blocked normal control techniques—any attempt I made to get in front of and around the shaft on my immediate right only led to Tiny trotting faster still, while pulling her head over would have meant pulling myself into the travois. The travois load rack was a menacing threat spread wide behind me and the situation turned desperate when Tiny broke into a canter. I was about to be run over by the load rack. Releasing the useless lead rope, I dove and rolled away to the left. The rack flew by beside me. I stood up slowly, checking for injury, and attempting to regain my composure. I was unhurt. Tiny was racing away at a panicked gallop with the travois bouncing wildly up and down behind her. She was headed for the fence gate where we had entered the pasture.

All I could do was watch and pray that the travois would neither fly apart (which would be a minor inconvenience) nor get tangled underfoot and cripple Tiny (which was a possibility too terrible to think about). Eventually, at the limits of my vision, Tiny pulled up sharply at the closed fence gate. I ran to catch up. When I reached her I found a wide-eyed pony with sweat-flecked, heaving flanks. She was unhurt and, when I inspected the travois carefully, I was surprised to find that it too was undamaged. It was good to know that horse and travois could stand up to a gallop, even if I could hardly credit myself on the way I had found out.

Standing beside Tiny, I worked to calm her, talking to her gently and massaging the soft ridge of tissue that roots the hairs of the mane. It took a long time before she relaxed. Then I took a deep breath and turned her out again toward the open pasture. We moved off at a slow walk. There was no doubt that both of us would rather have retired for the day, Tiny to some decent fescue, I to an appropriate drink, but I was unwilling to end the training session under the cloud of a near disaster. So, for another half hour we circled cautiously over the prairie without further incident. I never again tried any pace faster than a walk when on foot leading Tiny with travois.

The first time I mounted Tiny as she pulled travois was a leap into the unknown. As I swung into the saddle Tiny tensed and stepped briskly forward. With my legs splayed out around the shafts, the seating was both less secure and less comfortable than normal. The shafts rubbed on the inside of my thigh just above the knee, so the pressure contact between my upper leg and Tiny's flank, an important part of horse-rider communication and control, was lost. But travois travel was not such a dynamic event that this loss of contact was critical, and I raised the stirrups to take some pressure off the shaft-leg friction points. Once I was accustomed to mounted travois travel I experimented with the trot and canter, but, owing to the shafts, paces faster than a walk were too uncomfortable to use long term, and conveying both travois and rider at speed was hard work for Tiny.

We trained daily with travois, ranging through the valley bottomlands and up and down the hillslopes. Sometimes I was in the saddle; sometimes I led from the ground. Occasionally I ended a training run near the river and hitched Tiny's reins to a fence post so that I could enjoy a swim while she munched contentedly on the rich bottomland grass. But you should hitch a horse with a halter rope, not with the reins, and one day I paid for my sloppiness. Something startled Tiny as I slid the reins over a post and she jerked back so forcefully that the bridle leather ripped apart. I was astonished at her brute power; her disposition was so gentle that I sometimes forgot just how strong an animal she was. As she stomped back from the offending post I caught her easily enough, but it took several tries before I had the torn bridle tied well enough to get us home. Another lesson learnt: never go far on a horse without a spare bit of rope.

Every horseman or woman needs to know the proper use of rope. I had to learn the bowline, of course, with a quick release, and I also had to become familiar with proper hitches, but I was never to use the boy scout's favourite, the reef knot, the misuse of which is responsible for more deaths than all other knot misapplications combined. Years earlier I had been fascinated by a more obviously hazardous rope technique, the Spanish windlass, or "dead man's winch," once commonly employed to move heavy goods from ship to shore. Even today two people can use this technique to pull a heavy truck from a ditch, given a strong enough rope, a sound pole on which to wind the rope, and an immovable object to act as an anchor. Knot expert Ken Muggeridge had been reluctant to pass this dangerous knowledge on to me, and I remember the excitement of realizing the winch's leveraging power and the thrill of danger when I tried it out with a friend. As the rope creaked and groaned under tension, we backed off from testing the windlass principle to its limits, fearing a snapped rope or pole, and full of admiration for the sailors of old for whom the repercussions of a badly chosen or executed knot or winch could be deadly. The shipping, ranching, and many other rope-dependent trades have all changed and pass most of us by; now a failed knot means a loose shoelace or a lost shirt button. But I was happy to be dependent on a little basic rope craft, and there is solid satisfaction in the application of the right knot to the right job. This last skill mastered, I was ready to ride the valley.

CHAPTER SEVEN

" GEE UP ! "

OF A FINAL JOURNEY IN THE GREAT VALLEY & OF ADVENTURES WITH A PHILOSOPHICAL HORSE

ON A CLEAR MORNING in late June Tiny and I set out down-valley from Katepwa Lake. From my adventures with Serge I knew that it would be impossible to work a horse through the dense bush and marshy bottomlands of the eastern end of the valley, so with Tiny I hoped only to get as far as Crooked Lake. Sadly, we would be restricted largely to dirt-based, dry-weather byroads. With Serge I had been able to go through and under fence lines, and with the canoe, too, I had been independent of man-made trails, but a horse could be blocked by a single fence wire. It was not even practical to enter a pasture through a gate, for it was not normally possible to be sure what stock might be present, nor could I know where or if an exit gate lay ahead. So we would have to ignore inviting terrain behind even open fence gates and instead walk on or alongside the byroad that runs through much of the valley. With my anachronistic mind alive with images of a time when the Plains were unfenced, and truly Great, it was hard not to be saddened at this prospect.

A brisk headwind cooled our first steps. I alternated between riding Tiny and leading her, and was grateful for the choice. Walking was more work than you might think, for I had to maintain constant tension on the lead rope to keep Tiny stepping forward. It was tedious, but I could not fault her for her natural lack of enthusiasm at moving ever farther from home. Sometimes we walked on the pack-ed earth of the byroad, sometimes in the ditches alongside when the growth was

The old homestead

not too tall. But ditch walking was rough on the feet and there was always the danger of stepping on a hidden edge of steel or glass, for since the first roadside ditch was dug people have used them as casual drive-by garbage dumps. About once an hour a vehicle appeared. The driver always slowed to pass, partly out of curiosity and partly out of respect for horses. I found the going uneventful, bordering on dull, but it was the kind of day a horse finds fully satisfactory; it was only because I had the primate's overactive brain that I was dissatisfied. Tiny in fact had the day's only adventures. First she thought the noise and swivel action of a pumping irrigation nozzle clearly showed aggressive intent, and later she was panicked by a plodding cow, which, in Tiny's eyes at least, had snuck up on her from nowhere.

Late in the afternoon I pitched tent in open pasture across from an abandoned homestead. The unusually broad hay flat I stood on was the combined outwash from Smith and Price Coulees, parallel ravines opening out from the valley wall. The coulees were the source of the good spring water that had surely been the inspiration for the homestead. The site was aesthetic as well as practical, for the outwash flat was attractively framed by the north-slope hills behind it, and the coulees disappearing back into these hills provided just the right touch of landscape mystery.

It was not long before the local landowner turned up, drawn by that remarkable sixth sense that alerts farmers and ranchers to unheard and unseen strangers on their land. He proved very friendly and took me on a tour of the old homestead, including the abandoned farmhouse. Inside the house was classic prairie domestic debris: rotting upholstery, piles of old magazines and mail order catalogs, swallow and mouse droppings, and dust. Glass was everywhere—every single window pane had been shattered. A 1963 *Newsweek* featured the assassination of John F. Kennedy and spoke optimistically of the American military situation in Vietnam. A mattress label read "Regal Spring-Air Ltd. Winnipeg"—decaying evidence of the city's long upstream trading reach. Amid the melancholic mix of vandalism and neglect my guide pointed proudly to a startling, surreal object—a working telephone. Incredulous, I heard the warm purr of a dial tone. It was the only telephone for kilometres around; he maintained it as an emergency facility, especially valuable to the local public in winter.

Deeper water in the valley is often irony, but this homestead's well was excellent: shallow and with plenty of cold, sweet water under good pressure. I asked why the field I was camped in was unfenced, for it was obviously grazed by cattle later in the year. The pasture was large, he answered, and the coulees running through it made fencing very difficult. In the fall cattle did wander across the roadway and had on occasion been hit by the rare valley drivers, but only one or two people had ever complained.

All through my supper I peered into the mysterious coulees. With my hunger stilled, the will to explore rose inside me. Coulees always invite investigation. The bush can be too heavy to penetrate, but sometimes, if it has been dry, you can work your way up the streambed cut at the very heart of the ravine. Rock piles, shattered trees, and pools of stagnant water may all block this route, but the rewards can be wondrous: snakes, birdlife, the glint of mica or feldspar, an exposed soil profile bound in a maze of roots, animal tracks inscribed in mud, and, sometimes, sheltered by the deep coulee foliage from the prairie winds above, magical green stillness. Once I discovered great buffalo bones embedded in the sediment walls of a cut bank. I could identify a femur and a few vertebrae, the pitted bones of a single animal. When and how had it died?

Walking the coulee streambeds with a horse, even without a travois, would be impossible, so I took "the high road," intending to follow the coulee upstream by keeping just above the bush line. Tiny moved slowly through the cooling air of early evening as I angled her up the east wall of Smith Coulee. In places the slopes were too steep to ride, flatlander that Tiny was, and I had to dismount to lead her. Looking down, I could see deep into Smith Coulee. Fingers of green vegetation, rooted in the damp hollows of the coulee folds, reached up to spill over the valley edge and onto the great plain above. A little higher up, having reached the ridgeline dividing the two ravines, I could see into Price Coulee as well, an even steeper slash into the warm earth, the depths of its narrow wedge cloaked in solid aspen. On the coulee slopes, strewn among the bunchgrass, prairie lilies bloomed like living jewels, their ruddy orange so deep and rich that the colour would look a lie in a painting or photograph.

I was aware most of all of a great silence, broken only by the sputtering nasal *dzeeb* of the eastern kingbirds. This silence, combined with the huge sweep of my elevated vision, gave the landscape an edge of unreality, for the mind struggled with the paradox of so much land and sky and so little sound. A sharply defined frontal system arced across the western sky; its cirrus outriders looked timeless, frozen to the darkening blue dome of the heavens. When I turned Tiny around to start our zigzag descent back down to the valley floor, my mind too was in stasis; I felt transported back into a prairie ur-landscape. Tiny pulled me back to reality, for as we moved to cross the dirt roadbed at the foot of the hills, she tugged sharply westward. Granted freedom, she would have trotted hours through darkness to reach the comfort of familiar pastures and fellow horses.

Laypeople and horse experts alike argue as to whether horses are intelligent or not. Humans are impressed by the ability of horses to find their way home and to trace back journeys over great distances. Yet we are also contemptuous of their apparent ignorant cowardice when they start in alarm at an unexpected shadow, the sight of a cow, or a piece of paper blowing in the wind. The horse does have a sound, if pedestrian, mind for locking in memories of where there is good pasture and water. And its cognitive intelligence is real enough, but it is the nervous intelligence of a herbivore that has survived by its ability to escape predators by instant flight. The intelligence of dogs, by contrast, is of the hunting, searching, inquisitive kind, much more akin to human cognition and so more easily recognized by us. Like other herbivores, horses are conservative animals, not keen on adventures, aware that such foolishness typically leads not to pasture but to trouble. Horses are also sociable animals, fond of the company of their own kind, for they believe in security in numbers. Tiny's urge to turn for home was natural. Independent-minded though she was by equine standards, she was not looking forward to spending the night in unknown territory, on her own, without the help of other watchful horsey eyes.

I hitched Tiny to the free end of an eight-metre lead attached to a stake driven deep into the earth. At its top the stake was fitted with a free-spinning steel ring to prevent the lead from getting wound up or tangled. There was good grass and the grazing radius was big enough to keep Tiny occupied overnight. As I bedded down I could hear the nervous shuffling of hooves outside the tent. Several times I woke up in the night and listened through the tent wall. Never did I catch Tiny sleeping; always I heard her eating. Wary though she was, she did not forget her favourite activity.

Thunder was one reason for her watchfulness. It was to the south that night, but disquieting, for it made me question my wisdom in lying in an aluminum frame tent (stronger though it is than fiberglass) near a thunderstorm on the open prairie. Lightning is a strange power and more dangerous than many people think. We use the phrase "more likely to be struck by lightning" to suggest a probability so remote as to be worth discounting entirely, yet lightning kills some six hundred Americans a year. While your chance of a fatal strike would thus appear to be about two in a million per year, this is a misleading abstraction, for it lumps together those safe indoors in Toronto in winter with anyone unfortunate enough to be caught in a summer thunderstorm on the prairies, exposed and alone, a near two-metre-tall column of conductive water, the highest object around for miles. Caught outside in a storm, the technically correct advice is to squat low on the balls of your feet, rather than to lie flat on the ground, for most lightning deaths do not result from incineration by a direct strike, but rather from the current moving out from the strike point through the ground and through objects in ground contact.

A few weeks earlier I had witnessed a lightning strike close to me at Katepwa Lake. Examining the arboreal victim, I could follow the blackened and exploded bark that traced the route of the strike around and down the trunk and then on into the root system. A shallow crater of soil had been blown out around the root-stock. The injured cottonwood might yet live for the rest of the season, but the fluids of the sapwood had been superheated and vaporized, and the majestic tree, higher than its fellows, would likely die over the winter. In this most egalitarian of landscapes the strike seemed a just punishment for a tree that had dared to rise above its brethren: "Lo, how the mighty have fallen"—nowhere is this said with more satisfaction than on the prairies.

What I witnessed Herodotus had understood and used as powerful image-ry. He told of how Xerxes, an ambitious Persian king, was warned by a royal uncle not to let arrogance lead to unnecessary war: "You see how god strikes with his thunderbolts creatures that stand above the rest and removes them from his sight, but the small ones do not provoke him. You see how he is for-ever hurling his bolts upon the highest buildings and the tallest trees. For god loves to cut down all things that stand above the rest . . . For god suffers pride in none but himself."

Xerxes, foolishly, rejected the advice and was miserable in subsequent defeat, but I imagined that, given a voice, this blasted prairie cottonwood would not complain of its fate, for was not death by lightning in a great grassland thunderstorm as fitting a demise for a noble prairie tree as can be imagined? A strike is an even better fate for the true Plainsman or Plainswoman, for unlike trees, lingering mournfully after the blow, people usually either die quickly or recover completely. This compares very favourably with more mundane prairie accidents, like getting your arm caught in a grain auger.

The night's storm passed us by entirely. When we set off early next morning we enjoyed ideal travelling conditions: cloudy, with a light wind and occasional showers. The dampness was welcome, for it softened the ground and cushioned the steps of man and horse. Toward the end of the walking day we were able to strike off from the byroad and take up the old Hudson's Bay Company cart trail, for from my travels with Serge I knew it well enough to be sure its historic ruts would not leave us dead-ended. In the far distance, on the rich, black, alluvial soil of a potato field, four farm workers stood as stark silhouettes against the hills. The men appeared piteously tiny in the vast valley; their efforts, visible through binoculars, to move heavy irrigation lines by hand looked both noble and futile. It was an image from a Steinbeck novel: masculine, bleak, and shocking. Unusually, there were no vehicles anywhere visible. Without transport the men were, in the prairie sense, truly alone.

Upwind of us a mule deer watched our approach attentively, confused by the combination of horse and walker. We came surprisingly near before it broke into a brief stotting display. Fit the mulie might have been, but it allowed us too close; come hunting season it would be an ex-deer.

Inexplicably, wild animals are occasionally unwary of humans. Years earlier, while I was out walking a remote coulee ridge, a young whitetail doe had appeared ahead of me. She looked at me intently, then, despite being downwind of my scent, made a deliberate slow approach, her matchstick legs lifting and dropping delicately through the grass and shrub, until she was a mere six metres away. Her face radiated trust. As if this was not strange enough, the wail of a human baby sounded from deep within a nearby bush. The back of my neck tingled; the advance of the doe and the crying of a baby in the middle of nowhere were both bizarre; the fantastical idea occurred that the doe was coming to plead for help for the human child. Then, quicker than thought, the deer bolted, while in the bush the catbird (for that was what I had heard) altered its call cadence—and the spell was broken.

Leaving the cart trail, we turned onto a gravel road heading south toward Ellisboro crossing and the promise of good grass and ready water. The river was running low and the swallows were wheeling hungrily when we crossed over the bridge. A kilometre beyond the bridge we reached the two churches known to me from my dog travels. It was like visiting old friends when we stopped beside them for the night. In the hazy sunshine mountain bluebird fledglings pursued their parents around the churchyards, successfully begging for food. A favourite perch for the beautiful, shy songsters was the cross atop the Anglican church gable, from where the parents called to one another in a delicate *churrr*. I staked out Tiny and she dipped her head gently into the rich pasture, instantly absorbed in grassland recycling. A sparrow watched her with interest. From the farmhouse across the road a good-hearted gentleman emerged with a bucket of water, enough for myself and a small horse.

Water has always been a problem for prairie travellers. Exploring on foot in 1754 in the northern Plains, Anthony Hendry recorded in his diary on September 11: "The greatest hardships I have yet experienced is the Warmness of the weather, and the want of Water." In July of 1806, in the neighborhood of the Souris River, Alexander Henry wrote: "It sometimes happens in this country, in very dry seasons, that water is only to be found in some particular creek or lake. When this is the case we provide ourselves with small kegs or bladders. But this often proves insufficient; some people have lost their lives on this account, and others have had very narrow escapes."

European traders were astonished at the ability of Plains Indians to walk at speed for kilometres and days without water. What water there was was often of terrible quality and the traders marvelled at the necessary ability of the Native peoples to consume it. Eight days' journey beyond the Souris brought Henry into rugged country south of the Missouri, where he commented: "We suffered much from want of good water; that in the pond was a mere poison to the taste and smell, though the Indians drank it with pleasure. These savage brutes can drink stinking, stagnant water with as good a stomach as if it were spruce beer."

Other grassland peoples were as resourceful. The Querandí, after running down the Pampas deer in a death-by-exhaustion pursuit, drank thirstily of the life-giving blood of the chase. The Scythians of the western Steppes could live on mare's milk and, when the situation allowed it, ferment it into the alcoholic *koumiss* still appreciated today. The Mongols too travelled for days without water on their long journeys across the length of the thirteenth-century Steppes. Like the Scythians before them they lived on mare's milk or, if milk was unavailable, pricked a mare's neck vein and sucked horse blood until their thirst was quenched; kept within reason the blood loss would do the horse no harm. Sadly, the skills and endurance of Scythians and Mongols, or of Plains or Pampas Indians, were beyond me: I was an ever-thirsty product of the fluoridation age and sought my fluids from taps and filters.

Halfway up the south-slope hills a band of tall spruce embraced the grounds of Ellisboro cemetery. Once watered and rested, I left horse and churchyards behind and climbed toward the trees. I felt drawn to the cemetery's calm green beauty. Ascent complete, I stood in wonderment among the evergreens, thriving foreigners amid prairie grass. All around me, osmosis underground and tran-spiration above ground were raising water from root and soil to grass blade and spruce needle, from where the life-giving fluid was returned to the prairie sky. I felt myself, like grass and trees, metabolized by sun and air. From one dark spruce two juvenile great horned owls stared out, their eyes level with mine. Rufous, with down poking out all over, they were beginning the molt into adult greys. I searched carefully for parents and found a single imposing adult, high and distant in another tree, much more wary than the youngsters. I slowly approached to within fifteen metres of the juveniles. Their fluffy down made them look as big as adults and they already had the adult's dish face, set with aggressive yellow eyes, but as yet they lacked their identifying ear tufts.

From the cemetery I surveyed the churches and my horse below. Through binoculars I could see the arc sweep of a grazing horse's head, rhythmic and aesthetic, advancing slowly like a hand scythe through a rich harvest. I was too distant to hear the ripping sound of grass blade and root being torn asunder, and could contemplate with detachment the starch and sugar reprocessing under way below. Some modern ecologists like to suggest that the relationship between grazers and grasses is one of mutual gain, that grasses benefit from trimming, and that they grow rank and die in the absence of fire or grazing. Happy co-evolution of grazed and grazer, in a world of interdependent life-forms, is the flavour of our times. Yet the theory of mutual advantage is neither complete nor entirely false. On one remote Scottish island, red fescue grass, skeptical of co-evolving with grazers, has instead developed a symbiotic relationship with a fungus harmless to itself but toxic to grazing sheep. Be it by close-cropping sheep, root-tearing horse, or flesh-chewing human, aside from the occasional parasite or indestructible seed, passing through to better times, nothing really likes to be eaten.

Prairie plants and animals in fact work hard to avoid ending up as someone else's supper. The favourite tactic of the native grasses is to hide. Although their blades may rise only a few inches above ground, their root systems can drive down over decades to depths of two metres or more, and so ensure survival from grazing, fire, flood, or drought. Some small prairie mammals follow the grasses underground and live off the wealth of hidden biomass, while remaining themselves concealed from predators above.

To survive the winter cold, grasses and animals alike hibernate underground and under snow. Larger animals, like buffalo and deer, endure the winter topside, surviving by sheer size, their bulk and fat reserves seeing them through to spring. In the long winter nights sleep comes heavy to human prairie dwellers, as well as to the true hibernators, and we envy the birds their ability to forsake the northern grasslands for warmer points south. Like the grass and the ground squirrels, poorer people dig deep basements to survive the winter, while the wealthy fly south with the ducks and hawks.

Of those with cash or wings to flee, the true grasslands patriot is the Swainson's hawk, for when it leaves the prairies in fall its destination is the spring sun of the Pampas. Unable to hunt over the great tropical forests en route, some Swainson's arrive in the southern grasslands so weak that they can be picked up off the ground by hand. Those that survive their great migration are ill-paid for their grassland loyalty, for on the Pampas many fall victim to insecticide poisoning, and the number who live to return to the prairies is falling.

Still watching the grazing horse below, I was startled by the faint echo of a mainline train some eleven kilometres to the south. Hearing the train echo in the valley was a sign of a reflective cloud base, low and dense. Sure enough, dark clouds were massing not far to the west. By the time I had descended back to the churchyards the first raindrops were falling. They thickened into a heavy rain that persisted into the night, strong gusts snapping at the tent fly.

I was up before the invisible sunrise. The weather was unusual: very grey, with bands of mist hanging in the bush of the near-side hillslopes. A solid mass of fog cloaked the far side of the valley. Above us, two layers of cloud, one low and broken, one high and entire, completed our confinement. Wrapped in layers of humidity and cooled by a muggy north wind, we set off through a strange new world of constricted vision. With water underfoot and the grass and bush glowing deep green from the night's bountiful rain, the atmosphere was Plains Celtic; it was easy to imagine a leprechaun hidden in the bush, growing jealous and old over his buried pot of prairie gold.

The mud roadbed recorded a wealth of nocturnal toing and froing, especially of raccoon and deer. But the morning's heavy air muffled sound as much as sight, and the whole landscape seemed subdued. Very rarely, birdsong broke the silence. Tiny's four hooves had more trouble than my two feet as we trudged and slipped through the slick mud. She was especially leery of downhill slopes, for on descents the travois would slide forward and push her from behind. There were no vehicles on this mucky right-of-way today, since even the best four-wheel drive would soon have come to grief.

We ended the day's travels in a former schoolyard. The schoolhouse remained, but had long ago been converted into a rural community centre. The building looked run-down, almost ready to retire into abandonment, but there was still a lock on the door, so there was value in the structure yet. The yard was set some thirty metres above the valley floor at the foot of the north slope. Looking south over the valley, the view was grey mist and green vegetation, with blocks of fallow black. It was late afternoon and the world remained hushed. Even the mosquitoes had gone to ground, although an occasional swallow flew past in vain pursuit. The grass here was good and Tiny was pleased to be discharged of her load and staked out to graze. But she was tired from her muddy exertions and, after consuming a few mouthfuls, fell into a standing doze in mid-chew, grass stems poking out of her lips in all directions, reminding me of a farmer lost in contemplation of his wheat field. An old farmer, for as she entered into her dreams of horse Elysium, her muscles slackened, her head and lips drooped, and in a moment of time she aged years. I felt a protective instinct rise within me, together with affection. Silently I thanked her for her patient loyalty.

We both rested, then ate, and then rested again. The abutting slope hills, still wrapped in haze and mystery, called out for exploration to those recharged in body and spirit. Slowly we zigzagged up the steep inclines, ascending through patches of fog, until emerging onto the open plain above. From atop the great flatlands the north wind scudded mist and cloud over a gloomy valley; the view was arresting and bleak rather than beautiful. We turned and walked west along the valley edge to find cultivation pushed to the very lip of the slope, squeezing the last wheat plant possible out of the soil. Where the plough could not reach stood a stone pile, general rubbish, and rusted, abandoned, farm equipment. Discarded farm implements at valley's edge are a common sight; as a boy I had held the romantic notion that farmers were fond of their old equipment and upon its retirement wanted to reward its faithful work with a good view. Reality is purely utilitarian. Headlands, coulees, slopes, riverbanks—anywhere that cannot be ploughed to bring in a dollar—is a potential refuse site. Headlands are used as well to bury the dead of St. Lazare and Fort Qu'Appelle, although I had concluded at St. Lazare that the graveyard view was intentional and not merely an expedient use of wasteland.

Carefully we tacked back down the slopes to our campsite. When evening came the mist remained, transmuted by a strange, ocher tint. Smoke from the great forest fires of the north country, pressed by the polar wind, was drifting across the prairie, sinking into the silent valley, ominous and foreboding. Even as the smoke thickened, fine-grained drizzle filtered through, until the valley was murky with drifting carbon and water. An acrid smell permeated the haze. I imagined that I could even taste black bitterness in the air, although I might have been suffering the common sensory confusion of taste and smell.

There had been several spells of forest fire smoke in the valley this summer, sometimes drifting in from as far distant as the Northwest Territories. At times the sun had risen and set an angry crimson. But this was the densest smoke I had yet seen; I stood witness to far-away disaster. It was a reminder not only of another place but of another time, of the great prairie fires of old, when the flames flared from horizon to horizon, before roads and summerfallow parcelled up the danger into mere fragments of fire hunger. In ranching country, where roads and the plough are rare, cattlemen still sometimes search out a hill on a stormy night to watch for lightning strikes and grass fires. In earlier times prairie fire was a fearful threat to people and animals throughout the grasslands. In 1858 Hind reported on the burning of nearly the entire Canadian Plains:

> What a magnificent spectacle this vast prairie must have furnished when the fire ran over it before the strong west wind! From beyond the South Branch of the Saskatchewan to Red River all the prairies were burned last autumn, a vast conflagration extended for one thousand miles in length and several hundreds in breadth. The dry season had so withered the grass that the whole

country of the Saskatchewan was in flames. The Rev. Henry Budd, a native missionary at the Nepowewin, on the North Branch of the Saskatchewan, told me that in whatever direction be turned in September last, the country seemed to be in a blaze; we traced the fire from the 49th parallel to the 53rd, and from the 98th to the 108th degree of longitude. It extended, no doubt, to the Rocky Mountains.

Both Hind and Henry complained about Indians setting fires. Henry relayed reports of carelessness, while Hind recognized that the Indians often started grass fires deliberately. Like Hind, Daniel Harmon reported that the prairies burnt almost yearly, and after one blaze in 1805 he had great trouble finding pasture for his horses. For the Indians fire was a useful tool to drive the buffalo. It could also be used in war, or to drive away mosquitoes, and the new green grass that sprang up after rain on burnt prairie attracted buffalo. Of course, some fires ignited naturally from lightning strikes, and the Europeans themselves frequently set the grass-lands ablaze when their spark-spewing locomotives began crossing the prairies.

Although buffalo might benefit from fresh grass, in the first instance fire was a threat to them, for with their poor eyesight they often fell victim to flames and smoke. In November of 1804, on the Manitoba prairie west of the Red River, Henry came upon many buffalo burnt in a major fire. As he tells it, the survivors were more to be pitied than the dead: "Plains burned in every direction and blind buffalo seen every moment wandering about. The poor beasts have all the hair singed off; even the skin in many places is shriveled up and terribly burned, and their eyes are swollen and closed fast. It was really pitiful to see them staggering about, sometimes running afoul of a large stone, at other times tumbling down hill and falling into creeks not yet frozen over."

The buffalo regularly fell victim to water disasters too. They plunged through river ice, died mired in mud, or were swept away in the great spring floods. Descending the Qu'Appelle River in May of 1795, John Macdonell claimed in a single day to have counted 7,360 buffalo mired and drowned along or in the river. The carcasses, he said, "lay from three to five files deep." In April of 1801, at the Park River Post on the Red River, Henry watched the buffalo drift by in entire herds. "They formed," he wrote, "one continuous line in the current for two days and nights." A month later he complained: "The stench from the vast numbers of drowned buffalo along the river was intolerable." Hunters arrived to tell of the situation upstream of the post, leading Henry to write that "the number of buffalo lying along the beach and on the banks above passes all imagination . . . I am informed that every spring it is about the same."

If the elements sometimes destroyed the buffalo, the buffalo in turn wreaked havoc on the land. On migration they grazed and pounded the grass into above-ground oblivion, exposing the soil to the wind. If the land was wet, a million hooves churned and punched the prairie. Under a Plains sun the barren earth then baked and set into a foot-slicing wasteland of holes and mud spikes. In June of 1805 such a landscape left the men of the Lewis and Clark expedition limping and exhausted after their portage around the Great Falls of the Missouri. In the days of the buffalo, prairie waterways were often blighted by banks torn up by hooves and by shallows fouled with urine and excrement. My complaints about the impacts of European cattle on the modern prairie must, in the end, be put in this context. I may not like it, but the reek of river dung and the whine of biting flies are as natural to the prairie as sun, wind, and grass.

Fire, floods, and destructive grazing were only a few of the recurring catastrophes that defined the prairie environment. Grasshopper plagues, famed in prairie memory for the devastation they inflicted in the 1930s, are another natural and apocalyptic prairie phenomenon. In 1802 Harmon reported "incredible" and "astonishing" numbers of grasshoppers, which "devour every thing before them, scarcely leaving a leaf on the Trees or a blade of green Grass in the Plains." In 1808 Henry described grasshoppers dying in their millions in Lake Winnipeg; their decaying bodies gave off a "horrid stench." In the Souris River Valley in 1858, confronted with the grasshopper multitudes, Hind lost his professorial detachment:

Lying on my back and looking upwards as near to the sun as the light would permit, I saw the sky continually changing colour from blue to silver white, ash grey and lead colour, according to the numbers in the passing clouds of insects . . . The aspect of the heavens during the greatest flight we observed was singularly striking. It produced a feeling of uneasiness, amazement, and awe in our minds, as if some terrible, unforeseen calamity were about to happen. It recalled more vividly than words could express the devastating ravages of the Egyptian scourges, as it seemed to bring us face to face with one of the most striking and wonderful exhibitions of Almighty power.

Beyond grasshoppers and the much-cursed mosquitoes were other insect plagues. Hind observed armies of destructive caterpillars, while Henry complained of wood ticks. In May of 1801 Henry wrote:

. . . we have been plagued with wood ticks; and now that we are daily in the woods and grass, our clothes swarm with those troublesome and dangerous insects, which often get into the ear and cause inflammation. When they have time to get firm hold they cannot be removed without pulling the body from the head, which remains in the skin, and causes an itching which may last for several months. The bellies of our horses and dogs are covered with them; they adhere to the flesh until they have sucked themselves full of blood and are swelled nearly to the size of a musket ball.

Extremes and catastrophes define the Plains' sister grasslands too. In 1918 naturalist William Hudson described the "thistle years" of his Pampas boyhood, when giant thistles sprang up to create an impassable forest of spines, until they yielded in turn to the next disaster, burnt by a raging fire, or blown apart by the violent southwest storm wind, the *pampero*. In drought years on the eastern Steppes the herdsmen and women of modern Mongolia fight losing battles against the summer fires that destroy the thin grass pasture.

When you study the histories of the European settlers of the great grasslands you are witness to peoples trapped in cycles of environmental disaster. On the Canadian prairies in the winter of 1906-7 half the range cattle froze to death, destroying much of the young ranching industry forever. On the Pampas south of Buenos Aires fourteen million sheep were lost to floodwaters in 1900. Parts of the Plains were emptied of soil and pioneers in the great drought years of the 1930s. The thin soils of northern Kazakhstan, where Khrushchev's "virgin lands" plan put the Steppes to the plough in the 1950s, were lifted and lost to the winds of the 1960s. With their chronicles of catastrophe, how are we to understand the grasslands, sunlit breakers of dreams?

The grasslands are a spinning kaleidoscope of extremes, where "normal" has no meaning. Like Hudson on the Pampas, on the Plains, too, people are delivered from one extreme by the arrival of the next: an early bitter winter sees off an insect plague; a flooding thunderstorm breaks a drought. This is the spirit and reality of the grasslands, a reality fundamentally different to the temperate, stable environments of western Europe or eastern North America. It is no wonder that so few people of European mind have ever been able to accept the prairies on the land's own terms. But those who strive for a controlled, predictable life on the grasslands, who try to replicate the spirit of gentler lands, are doomed to incomprehension and frustration.

In the half-light I wrote my judgments of people and prairie:

> In my country,
> the railway, the horse, and the dog are forgotten;
> metal boxes, made in Japan, roll between the wheat fields,
> and the Indian lies shunted on a siding.

> In my country,
> the sun shines hot and cold;
> the grass burns and bends, till bitten by the snow,
> and the north wind blows life away.

In my country,
the people are rich and fat;
they complain, sit blind, eat deeply,
but when old they embrace the land.

In my country,
the sky-dome sits on grass;
the trees rise burnt and dry,
and nowhere can you hide from God.

Hidden in my tent from the gloom and damp, I drifted into an uneasy sleep, only to awaken to drizzle, smoke, and a struggling dawn. I tried to roust body and mind with an ambitious plan to strike out in search of challenge and adventure, but it took all my weakened powers of self-motivation to break camp under these dismal conditions. Yet as horse, travois, and man moved off in the murk, the haze was beginning to lift. My mind cleared away smoky contemplations to deal with the day's decisions.

A local farmer had informed me of an old wagon trail that ran along the foot of the north-slope hills. It was, he thought, passable with a horse. There was a fall-back plan too. Should the trail prove blocked, it was also, he had assured me, possible to make headway along the valley's edge atop the north slope. I was skeptical about both routes, but I was now bored with the valley floor byroad and keen to test the limits of horse and travois travel. We would try the wagon trail and take things as they came.

At first the trail was clear and we made good progress, but after an hour it petered out in a field of dense alfalfa. It was impossible to go any farther. The smoke had lifted almost entirely, but the drizzle continued, and the north wind had strengthened. I stood and considered. Then, rejecting retreat, we turned sharp left and pushed through a corner of alfalfa toward the shortgrass slopes of the hills. The cut to the slopes was short, but the hay was heavy with rain and dragged on my legs, as if to emphasize my guilt at walking through standing crop. Finally, on six soaked legs we reached the freedom of shortgrass. We paused briefly and then attacked the slope straight up, breaking for breath when Tiny stalled behind the lead rope. At each pause I spoke to her, praising her strength, as she exhaled vapor and heat. On the final assault she herself took the initiative and powered over the top of the valley with a grunt of achievement.

The satisfaction of accomplishment faded quickly. Visibility was poor, but what I could see made the fall-back route look doubtful from the start. Bush, thick in the folds of the hills, pushed up to, and sometimes over, the lip of the valley. The critical question was whether we would be able to go around the topland bush encroachments or whether a fence line would squeeze us into the scrub. The wind whistled over the valley edge, driving a cold rain down my neck. I led off, shivering and pessimistic.

Not without cause. Sure enough a fence line appeared, running close to the valley edge in pursuit of every possible blade of pasture. Twice we managed to squeeze through where scrub pushed up to the fence line, but our victories were those of the gambler about to lose all, for on our third such attempt the travois wedged solidly amid bush and twisted trees. Tired, and with my fingers stiff from the cold, I struggled to first unhitch the travois load, then to unhitch the travois from Tiny, and finally to work by hand both load and travois back out of the bush. Manoeuvering the travois was awkward, for its projecting crossbars caught and held on every branch or root with devious skill and tenacity. Having passed from grassland into forest, the travois came alive with duplicity, its wooden heart determined to re-root itself among its uncut kin. Cursing its willfulness, I finally wrestled the travois back out into grass, where it turned quiescent, feigning death. The battle left me scratched and bruised. Across the fence line the pasture lay close-cropped and empty, ideal for travois travel. Three strands of wire barred the way, mocking me.

Many technological innovations have altered the face of the prairie, but none more fundamentally than barbed wire. Before its invention fencing was impossibly expensive in the open West and cattle, people, and wild animals roamed free on a great common. When, amid an explosion of barb patents, the production of cheap barbed wire was perfected in the late 1870s, the parcelling, sale, and partition of the grassy heart of North America could follow. As I lamented my plight, stranded on a remnant patch of native prairie, the doomed plea of the cowboy wheeled uselessly in my head: "Don't fence me in!"

I returned to Tiny, who stood patiently in the bush, and assured her that my curses had not been directed at her. Having been led into a dead-end tangle by demonstrably poor leadership, she was understandably unimpressed at now having to retrace what she knew to be a difficult route. But there was no other option. Slowly I talked her back out of the bush. On open grass I rehitched the travois and we set off on our long westward retreat. Carefully we rethreaded the bush where it pushed up to the fence. Finally we reached the corner where the fence line turned due north. We turned with it and trudged away from the valley, north across fallow mud, skirting the low and marshy hollows, searching vainly for a firmer track, great clods of mud falling from our every foot and hoof.

Our current navigation problems were only a dim echo of those that once faced travellers on the prairies, for while we encountered barriers to travel, I was never truly lost, adrift in the grass, devoid of all orientation and threatened by Plains madness in a land of endless horizons. Spanish-speakers have invented a word for this danger: *empamparse*, to become lost and disoriented on the Pampas. Travelling the open prairie, even between secure sources of water and shelter and along a known route, was a risky venture in earlier days. It was riskier still for those who struck out in ignorance of what lay ahead, like the first Europeans: Coronado, Kelsey, La Vérendrye. How bold La Vérendrye and his men must have been to set out in 1738 from the Assiniboine River in search of the Missouri! It was a great prairie traverse into the unknown. Hubert Smith asserted rightly: "The journey must have seemed at times to the French like an ocean voyage, with little beside the sun and stars for useful reference points." *Empamparse* has a fitting secondary, figurative meaning: to be amazed.

While La Vérendrye and his party journeyed on foot, travellers used horses when available. In 1877 U.S. army colonel Richard Dodge described the difficulties of Plains navigation from the horseman's point of view. On the level Plains the principal problem was the lack of landmarks—in such a landscape travel really was akin to voyaging the high seas. On the other hand, in more rugged country, especially in "badlands" country, it was easy for a rider to become lost in the myriad windings of gullies and ravines, and it was easy, too, to become stranded in a box canyon with no exit for horse or rider.

Dodge identified the asymmetry of the navigation problem within ravine systems. Moving down-valley or down-canyon, the direction of necessary progress is clear, and a camp or meeting place located down-valley is always easily found simply by travelling with the flow of the valley or river at every junction. Navigation up-valley to a specified point is much more difficult, for at every valley junction the traveller must choose which branch to follow up and which to ignore; the possibilities for error are as many as the tributary ravines. In general, Dodge advised against up-valley travel unless the country was well known to the traveller. He instead recommended riding the ridges between watersheds wherever possible, in effect observing the mountain walker's old dictum of never giving up altitude unnecessarily. On the prairies many useful ridge routes were already well marked by buffalo trails before serving as pathways for horse and rider.

Any traveller over irregular natural landscapes soon learns that straight-line travel is rarely the shortest distance between two points. Yet maintaining your sense of direction on twisting trails is difficult. It is true that in some wooded country moss prefers the (damper) north side of trees. It is also the case that leaves tend to be larger on the (cooler) north side of a broad-leaved tree. But Prairie grasses offer only the undependable hint of tending to be bent in the direction of the prevailing wind. Prairie travellers had to navigate by sun and stars, by memory, or, most accurately, by compass. Dodge recorded cautionary stories of those disoriented travellers who trusted their compass against all the intuition of their senses, and lived to tell about it, and of those who disbelieved their compass, and paid the price.

At times maintaining the high ground was impossible and a river crossing had to be undertaken. Governor Simpson found himself and a few companions in this unhappy situation in May of 1825. From Carlton House, on the south bank of the North Saskatchewan River, Simpson set out overland by horse to the Red River settlement (present-day Winnipeg). En route he had to cross the Qu'Appelle River. Just as I experienced on my Qu'Appelle crossing with Serge, the reluctant husky, Simpson had mosquito troubles. But he also had serious horse problems:

> . . . the Water was too Deep to Wade, there was no Wood of any kind to make a Raft Several of our people could not swim and the bottom and banks so soft that there was the utmost danger of drowning or miring our Horses; in this dilemma we had nearly resolved on Killing our Horses & making Skin Canoes of their Hides for the purpose of going down to the Settlement by Water I however being more at home in the Water than any of my fellow Travellers and anxious to save the lives of the poor animals stripped and Swam across with a few things 3 others followed my example and by making several crossings in this way we got the whole of our little Baggage over; the Horses were driven across those people who could not Swim holding on by their Tails and with the assistance of Cords we hauled the poor Animals out of the Mud . . . nearly the whole of which time myself and those with me being naked in the Mud & Water exposed to the blood thirsty assaults of Miriads of Muschetoes, in short I believe there never was an unfortunate Govr in such a Woeful plight as that of the Northn Deptmt of Ruperts Land this Day.

Although I felt almost equally mired in farm field mud, no Simpsonesque ingenuity was needed, just perseverance over an awkward route. I knew roughly where we were and could make a good guess as to the length of the required detour. But it was slow going and the wind and rain kicked straight in our faces. With every step the mud clutched and tugged at our legs. I was wise to have packed a toque, for although spared the attacks of mosquitoes, I was now as soaked and chilled as Simpson had been after his Qu'Appelle crossing. Tiny plodded on resignedly, head bent deep.

Finally the fence line to our right ended its northward run and turned east again. We turned with it, following an east-west farm trail. Now we were side on to the rain, a much more comfortable orientation. Psychologically I was boosted as well, for we were again moving in the right direction. When the muddy track arced south to descend into the valley, I turned almost cheerful. Below the valley's edge there was shelter from the north wind and, even through the drizzle, the view across the curving sweep of the valley was spectacular in its scale. We descended cautiously, tacking where necessary to give Tiny a firmer grip on the hillside mud.

Once we were returned to familiar valley bottomlands, it was straightforward work to continue east along a valley byroad. But the day's exertions had left us both on the edge of exhaustion. I was relieved to spot a cropped hay flat, well edged with bush. We pulled in and I immediately pitched tent close to the sheltering scrub. Then I crawled into my sleeping bag, keen to conserve heat and recharge a drained body. As I zipped down the tent fly, Tiny stared at me accusingly. For the first time I had staked her out in something less than the superb pasture she reckoned was her due. I was too tired to even mentally apologize. She made do, for even as I drifted into a doze I heard the sundering of grass from earth and the rhythmic music of cellulose ground between molars.

The next morning dawned dry and fine. It was not far to our destination, the provincial park at Crooked Lake. Because of fences the only feasible route forward for Tiny would take us alongside the paved highway that skirts the north edge of the lake. I was leery of traffic and public attention, so I decided to cache the travois at the hay flat and to reincarnate Tiny as a packhorse. This she accepted without complaint and we set off for the lake. The going was easy and the few car drivers we met at this early hour were invariably courteous. It was not long before we saw open water. The cottages dotted along the lakeshore were small and sympathetically sited, with the exception of a few A-frames ugly enough to figure as targets for aesthetic terrorism. In fact cottage country made for pleasant walking, for we could often follow quiet service tracks away from the highway. Children were thrilled to see and speak to Tiny, as were a few adults, although the latter were shyer in their interest.

I wish I could report meeting the same affection upon arrival at the park gates. To my disbelief, I was informed that government policy did not allow horses in the park. It was profoundly depressing to encounter such institutionalized disdain for our prairie roots, where even in the few public corners of prairie spared from agriculture, the horse is unwelcome. To deal with our immediate needs for grass and water, I bargained out a compromise with the gatekeeper. This allowed Tiny to remain in the park for a few hours, *so long as she was hidden from public view.* Lord forgive us—that children of the Great Plains would take offense at the sight of a horse!

Subdued, I led Tiny into the centre of a bluff of trees and there staked her out on a patch of grass. On behalf of all grassland people of good will I apologized to her for this shameful ostracism. She wasted no time in reflection, instead bending down to tear the grass from the good earth below. From many kilometres away an internal combustion engine would soon be racing to meet us at unhorselike speed. Our truck transport would return us and travois home to the hillslopes of Katepwa Lake in a journey without dignity. Encased in our respective metal boxes, we would roll over a strip of asphalt hot-poured and frozen on the living earth. Oh, for the unfenced prairie! How much we have lost!

AT KATEPWA I began my retreat from the past. In our last travois days Tiny pulled children on the load rack across the prairie, just as Indian horses before her had pulled the young or infirm. The children found a walking pace comfortable, if a bit dull. At a trot their bones bounced against the rack cross-poles, while at a canter the ride was surprisingly smooth as the shaft ends flew up and skidded off the ground, just as an inner tube pulled by a powerboat will skip across the water from wave crest to wave crest. Of course, the consequences of falling off the load rack at speed would be more severe than bouncing from a rubber tube into water. But youth is sensibly unconcerned by such details, and the youngsters enthused about the speed and excitement of the canter. It was "Better," they said, "than the rides at the exhibition."

After these final experiments I retired the travois, respectfully, and rode Tiny deep into the fall, savouring every day. Prairie perfection seems close enough to touch on some autumn days, when the frost has swept flies and mosquitoes into memory, the fields lie cropped or fallow—open to horse and rider—and the pure morning air hangs chilled and sharp. And the light: on a clear morning in late September it can be of disconcerting clarity. The mind, too, is cool and lucid after the heat and hurry of the short prairie summer.

Much of a man's joy for life is squeezed out of him by social constraints, be they sensible or petty. I know of no better cure for a cramped personal world than a horse. Like the Plains Indians and many other liberated footmen before them, I stepped up by the stirrup into instant nobility, proud and confident. Across the open West we would gallop, flying as fast as ever man dreamed of moving before the industrial age. Sometimes we climbed out of the valley to follow the edges of the coulees as they threaded far out into the plains north and south. From the toplands we spied down at owls and deer hidden in the coulee bush below. When we moved away from coulee's edge all sense of scale was lost, the prairie vastness opened to receive and engulf us, and our progress was an endless march on an infinite plane, with an ever-receding horizon before us. This was the freedom of the frontier, the hinterland, the great beyond, that the bold have aspired to always. It was the freedom of the Spanish *peón* throwing Old World hierarchy to the four winds of the Pampas; in mounting a horse he was elevated in status as in physical fact and became a *caballero*—the Spanish fusion of "horseman" and "gentleman." It was the freedom, too, of the American frontiersman, moving ever west to new lands, and of the Russian Cossack, a gallop ahead of the tsar's power and authority. By day the Cossack spoke the old freeman's boast of independence: *"Moskva daleko otsyuda"*— "Moscow is far away"— and by night he slept free. Fragments of Nikolai Gogol's tales of Cossacks in the tallgrass Steppes flowed through my mind: "All that was dim and drowsy in the Cossacks' minds flew away in a twinkling: their hearts fluttered like birds. The farther they rode, the more beautiful became the steppe . . . In those days all the south . . . was a green, virgin wilderness. No plough had ever passed over the immeasurable waves of wild growth; horses alone, hidden in it as in a forest, trod it down. Nothing in nature could be finer . . . Oh, how beautiful they are, the steppes! . . . 'Look, children! Yonder gallops a Tatar . . . You would never catch him in all eternity; he has a horse swifter than my Devil.'"

Sunrise and sunset were the most magical moments. On a calm day with horizon cloud it was like watching a great painter experimenting with a palette of colours, liberated from the conventions of scale and modesty imposed by lesser landscapes. But as much as the magnificence of the mounted view, it was, as at Smith and Price Coulees, the absence of sound in the great open plain that struck deepest in the mind; it seemed impossible that the world could be so vast and yet be silent. The spell would be broken by the rustle of a sparrow, or by the draining of colour into the greys of dusk, or by the white light of advancing dawn. The strange magic gone, the belly was left aching with wonder.

One sun-swept afternoon I approached Tiny in open pasture to catch her for our final ride together. As always, she trotted briskly away for a few steps, perhaps out of excitement, perhaps to show me she could run free if she chose to. Talking softly to her, I caught her, and saddled up. Slowly we headed up the slopes for a last exploration of coulee country. Above us, a V-skein of geese moved silently down-valley, each goose riding the updraft spinning from her companion's leading wing tip. Great white pelicans, returning from a day on the lakes, followed; the slow synchronized beat of pelican wings flowed like a graceful sine wave down the thread of individuals in flight. A hare, confused in both mind and colour, stared at us nervously, then fled as we passed; its body was still brown, but its ears and the undersides of its feet shone pure white. As evening approached it occurred to me that Tiny was indifferent to the wonders of colour now flowing over the sky with the setting of the great prairie sun, they were so much a part of her everyday life. When I turned her to return down the valley slopes she moved willingly, keen for a trot to take her home quickly. Near valley bottom we moved across a coulee mouth. A river of cold air, draining from the cooling plains above, flowed down and thickly over us; I shivered in the immersion. Around us the autumn prairie grew in mystery as the dusk deepened and perfect stillness settled over the land. The promise of moonrise glowed cold and faint on the eastern horizon. I unsaddled Tiny and set her free to pasture. She trotted off into near darkness. Then, just as years before when I had stared into the sky's fading light from the glass dome of a train car, I was alone in a landscape of the mind.

CHAPTER EIGHT

DAY FLIGHT

OF HOME AND THE VIEW FROM ABOVE

SO ENDED my valley journeys, with the mystery of the evening breeze sinking away into the dried-up grasses of a darkening prairie. Don Gayton, a modern Plains vision-seeker, writes of lying in a prairie blowout, hoping the wind-cut hollow will transport him to the visions of a Blackfoot dreamed. I too had hoped to attain some of the old wisdom of grass, wind, and sky.

Did my white predecessors in the valley, the traders and explorers from the East, discover wisdom in the grasslands? Daniel Harmon, a deeply religious man, found his faith troubled, not enriched, by years of fur trade isolation. Alexander Henry, of more robust character, was at ease in the prairies, but largely restricted his writings to the business of the fur trade. He neither sought nor gained insight into the land beyond commercial acumen. Henry Hind was a developer prospecting the wealth of the land for agriculture and industry. His notes reflect this preoccupation. These three are representative of the majority of white traders and explorers; they came to the prairies for material gain and for the love of adventure. Beyond these ends they sought no wisdom and were uninterested in the beliefs of the Indians, except insofar as they affected business. Confident of his own religion, Hind wrote of those of the Indians only in passing and always dismissively: "In the valley of the Qu'Appelle River, we frequently found offerings to Manitou or Fairies suspended on branches of trees; they consisted of fragments of cloth, strings of beads, shreds of painted buffalo hide, bears' teeth and claws, and other trifles . . . Like most heathen and barbarous races, Indians suffer much from their superstitious fears." The moral certainties of Hind's Victorian age that allowed him to condemn the practices and beliefs of others so confidently have long since collapsed behind us. Today most of us, Native or non-Native, are uncertain of heart.

On one journey I climbed up the valley's north slope at Crooked Lake and searched out the great Indian burial mound at valley's edge, built centuries before the coming of the horse, on a site and in a style Schevchenko would have approved of. Our backs to the flatlands, the mound and I looked out over the valley and lake below, the hillslopes falling away at our feet. The untiring wind blew behind, around, and beyond me. Before me the slope grasses bent, stood tall, then sighed and bent again, paying endless homage to the wind. Try as I might, I received no special wisdom from this very special site. Weariness and disappointment were my companions as I returned to the valley below. Perhaps I lacked the physical hunger to match my spiritual craving, for many vision-seekers work on an empty stomach. But I carried the modern fondness for regular food, and deep in my spirit was the impatience of the modern age. Most commonly I found that the end of a hard day of travel led not to insight but only to a harvest of aching muscles and deepest sleep.

Yet if I confess to attaining no "higher state" of knowledge through my journeys, I must equally add that I am not discontented with this outcome. Many philosophers have long maintained that life is a journey, not a destination, a view I am sympathetic to, for from the beginning the point of my journeys was the travelling, rather than the arriving. And I have never held the romantic notion that the world is explicable.

Even so, I am not so modest as to deny all claim to learning from my adventures. There were indeed a few epiphanies on my journeys, though never when I was consciously striving after insight. Loneliness on the prairie I found to be a necessary tribulation on the road to discovery, a joyous and exquisite torment akin to that felt as a boy peeling off an old scab to reveal the wonder of fresh, raw flesh below. When my mind was empty of striving and worry and desire—and simple physical exhaustion could be a great aid in this—then, sporadically, I could see into the prairie. There was no need for a church or its like to mediate the spiritual world; the open land and sky were heaven undiluted.

So it was that one day, tired and alone, and with a mind washed empty by the purity of the prairies, I understood how the deserts of the Old World had fired and sustained the great monotheisms, for the clarity and simplicity of a desert—or of a desolate plain—persuade you that the universe is made up of but one God. The only plausible prairie alternative, that you stand irredeemably solitary, turned completely on yourself in an endless, empty landscape, is too terrible to contemplate.

More often than toward understanding, the scale and beauty of valley and prairie moved me to awe. In this I was in good company, for all writings of those who lived and travelled the early prairies are somewhere marked with landscape awe and astonishment. Moments of wonder were a serendipitous reward for traders seeking their living in a strange land.

The essence of prairie, which is a combination of grand scale on the one hand and landscape subtlety on the other, is immensely difficult to convey by words put to paper. The root problem is not that the land itself defies description. The difficulty is that the grasslands are a feeling more than a view. It is this sensation, our powerful emotional response to the prairie landscape, that confuses and eludes definition or understanding. It is equally difficult to define the experience of the grasslands' doppelgänger, the sea. The ocean waves and the prairie grasses both bend and curl at ease with the wind; the mystery lies in us and it is ourselves we struggle to comprehend adrift on sea or grass.

To the invading whites, the prairies seemed like an open canvas, blank and unscripted, a landscape ripe for molding to human purpose, whether by individualist or communalist, Ukrainian or Scot. This reading of the land, encouraged by governments seeking settlers to the West and still dominant in the minds of many prairie dwellers, could not be further from reality. It is the old Indian lifestyles that provide clues to an accurate reading of the land and of how to live with its unpredictability. Consider the Ojibwa reaction to one of the prairie catastrophes that so troubled the newcomers. In 1857 Hind wrote: "The Indians had seen the grasshoppers before, but never in such alarming numbers; they appeared, however, quite indifferent to their progress, and quietly amused themselves as they squatted or lay on the ground, by jerking the intruders off their arms and legs with a thin piece of wood, bent by the fingers so as to act as a spring."

The Plains Indians, swift and flexible, and demanding little of the land, had no reason to be alarmed by the latest grasslands plague. They shared the Pampas Querandí lifestyle described by Father de Ovalle two centuries before Hind's prairie travels. How could material tragedy reach peoples with so little material dependence? On the Steppes, too, life was simple and mobile, and the pastoralists knew to bend like the grass with the wind and to move with the rain and the seasons.

Under its nomadic inhabitants the Steppes survived millennia, until the Marxist variant of European materialism stretched eastward, cut up the virgin pasture into huge farms, and brought the disasters of the plough and central planning. The Pampas fell to great cattle barons and then to wheat. The American and Canadian "national dreams" required farmers, too, and by the hundreds of thousands they came, lied to about life on the Plains. Many immigrants hated the reality of the prairie and many left or, like Tom Sukanen, died with their hearts in another land.

How wonderful it would be if we were to accept the catastrophic nature of life on the grasslands in the manner of their original inhabitants, viewing each landscape revolution with equanimity or exhilaration! How sad it would be if the prairies worked the way we wanted them to, like the soft lands of eastern North America or western Europe, where the seasons cycle gently and the rains hardly ever fail! Yet the day of reconciliation seems far off, for we still struggle to reduce the prairies to foreign norms of environmental constancy. Everything in our culture seems to demand control and predictability from the land. At every failure to assert our dominance, another wave of people leaves the prairie. Left behind in "next-year country" is a populace skewed to the stubborn, the old, and the irrationally optimistic, bonded by a mistrust of eastern banks and the weather.

Sometimes I see a home on the prairie standing exposed to grass and wind, without the good-citizen badge of shelterbelt trees planted round it, and I wonder if those living inside are on the road to prairie reconciliation. They have rejected the foreign vision of trees and gardens on the open prairie—you can see the Ontarian version of the eastern ideal preserved at the Motherwell homestead just north of the Qu'Appelle Valley—in favour of the reality of the land. Discarding the baggage of treeism is only one adaptive step, and arguably a foolish one, perhaps rooted in apathy, for shelterbelts trap snow moisture and cut heating costs, but I admire the new Plainsman or woman who is at ease without trees.

Our lifestyles are startlingly new and unproven in this biblical landscape of floods, droughts, insect plagues, and fire-bolts from heaven. We live here like tourists "just passing through," with the tourist's eye for a quick bargain. We pull potash, oil, and water from deep underground, strip coal from the surface, and mine the soil above with wheat and corn. It is a cut-and-run economy worked in reflex to the changing demands of markets far away. Small towns on the prairies are like offshore oil platforms, temporary resource-extraction communities isolated in a hostile environment. Of course it is impossible for modern prairie people to break away from the controlling economies of the populous heartlands, even if we wanted to. Though few in numbers, we are still far too many to make a living without struggling against the climate and mining the land.

Against this stands the fact that we cannot "tame the West." The concept is as flawed as the old snake-oil chant that "rain follows the plough," the fantasy that lured thousands of settlers to personal catastrophe. Travelling the valley, I saw the remains of ambition and dreams: wood skeletons of schoolhouses bent and split by wind and frost, and abandoned homesteads with their green cloaks of hedge and trees hanging on longer than their creators. These places, not clean white churches, are the spiritual centres of European civilization on the prairies.

They are remnants destined to be sucked dry, flattened and scattered by prairie wind, and then buried by prairie grass.

We are still too new to the prairie and too busy with day-to-day life to comprehend the land's slow power to reclaim its own. We are heirs of a prairie well ploughed and fenced and are blind to our great grassland heritage. A few prairie dwellers lament the passing of the open grasslands in all their majesty: the surging herds of great mammals, the birds alighting in their millions, the blaze of the great fires. They are right to grieve; what we have destroyed was worth more than wheat or oil. Yet it is not the natural world so much at risk here as ourselves. Our trees will die, and the immortal grasses will return to heal the scars of homesteads and garbage, and in time the animals and birds will follow. Fire and flood will cover the land again. But what kind of people will be living here then?

AS A CLOSING HOMAGE to the prairie and valley I wanted to share the view with the hawks I had so often admired from below on my journeys. The grasslands have always been exceptional territory for winged and feathered hunters. Game may be sparse, but the raptor's sharp eye can sweep vast hunting fields with casual efficiency. As thermals, the transmuted power of the summer sun, spiral upward, their energy is seized by the wings of soaring hawks, eagles, and vultures. Life, viewed from below, looks easy and free in perfect prairie skies.

From a small airplane, climbing up to nine hundred metres, the prairies grew in greatness; even as they fell away beneath the plane's wing, their scale remained infinite. The aircraft was a riveted box of noise and vibration, an unnatural contraption that Lucifer himself might have invented to tempt us to defy God's division of the winged from the heavy-footed. But oh, the view from heaven, open and boundless, was strong magic; to share the eagle's vision Satan could have had my soul that day.

The geometry of square fields and arrow-straight roads was boldly modernistic and overwhelming in its impact, like a Mondrian painting gone mad in scale. Into this structured world the great valley cut inexplicably; it seemed, contrary

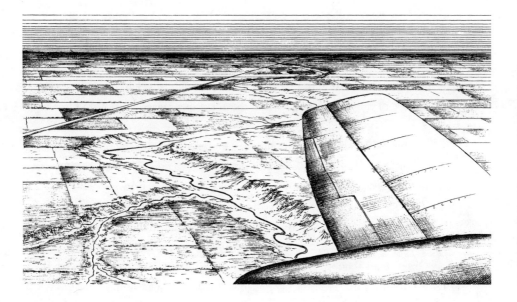

The Plains from above

to reality, that the valley must have come after the Mondrian, the confounding slash of some giant vandal tormented by modern abstractionism. Then the Quaternary came into focus, the hummocks and hollows of glacial rubble strewn across the plain. The dead weight of ice had ground across this land, spitting out multi-tonne boulders and dust-milled granite plucked from the stony lands far to the north. When the frozen ocean itself cracked and crumbled, roaring walls of water flowed out, sculpting rock-dust and boulder alike, then sinking below to uncharted aquifers, artistry complete. Nearly every natural feature I could see was the work of water, whether cold and stiff or liquid magic. With wonderment I traced the shoreline of a long-dry lakebed. Within its bounds the soil was silty and rich and on the fallow the earth tones spoke of moisture or aridity, of success or failure in next year's crop. The twisting valley coulees fingered far to the north and south, inviting the prairie waters down to the Qu'Appelle. Alluvial fans spread at the mouth of every coulee; those that ended in the lakes were curled to the east. Like refugees from the dust bowl thirties, bush and trees poked cautiously from the coulees into the open plain above, holding tenaciously to every crevice, or hollow, or north-facing slope, and avoiding exposure to the desiccating sun and wind of the flatlands. It was a remarkable marriage of human and natural landscapes, of the straight-edged and the curvilinear, each beautiful in its own way, each oblivious to the aesthetic of the other.

As the immigrants found, it can take a long time to learn to love the prairies, if you ever learn at all. But love for the grasslands, when you have it, is a deep joy. In this the grasslands are not unique; lands and waters everywhere and always can work their way into our hearts, if we are willing to be open to their magic. The price of the love of place that results is a dependence that grows as we age, as rootedness displaces adaptability. The price is more than fair.

Great cloud-shadows drifted east across the land. As the plane banked to the right, sunlight glittered from the precious thread of river below. Memories and emotion flooded through my mind, of days and nights with dog and horse and dragonflies, of buffalo dreams and mosquito mornings. I thought of poor Tom Sukanen, stranded and buried on the prairie lands below, and I felt a pang of his fatal homesickness; my ambition of soaring above the valley now realized, I yearned to be back afoot in the coulees. *"Qui appelle?"* the old travellers asked the echoing valley walls, and now I knew the answer. As some land, somewhere, calls to each of us, the valley was calling me home.

Acknowledgments

ON THE PRAIRIES it is difficult to survive alone, and I surely could not have completed my research or journeys without the help of many people. I am above all grateful to Jim and Elaine Tomkins for entrusting me with Serge and to Errol Cochrane for loaning me Tiny. I thank the Fates that I was able to return both companions safe from their travels.

Rob Woodward, Paul Pichette, and Lorne Millar shared parts of my journeys or training. I learned much from each of them. Heidi Martin, Wes Stewart, Chris Skinner, Chad Skinner, Penny Pedersen, Randy Teed, Kirk Cochrane, and Chris and Grace Pedersen were all sources of equestrian learning. Derek Hawken and Brian Martin rode the horse travois load rack. Frank Mymryk and Don Pinay advised on huskies. For academic council on a range of topics I am indebted to John Pomeroy, Valeri Neronov, E. Milner-Gulland, Zoheir Abouguendia, John Biggart, Mikhail Semenov, Dean Smith, Charles Watrall, David Miller, Margaret Hanna, Ernest Burch Jr., Grace Morgan, Marvin Kay, Brian Fagan, Darryl Adamko, Doug Conway, Sheldon McLeod, and several anonymous readers for the Center for American Places. For comments on drafts or for help with practical aspects of this book I gratefully acknowledge the contributions of David Hallam, Robert Cook, and Elaine Barrow (all of whom provided constructive comments on complete drafts), Greg Marchildon, David Wishart, Brian Mlazgar, Jay Armstrong, Sheila Davies, Patrick Douaud, Jeanne Shami, James McCrorie, Nick Carter, and J. Clark Archer. For logistical assistance I thank Ted Duce, Herb Jack, Kevin Bolianatz, Peter Ashcroft, Lee and Terry Eisler, Meg Millar, Stewart Bengart, Lee Heinrich, Marianne Weston, Allan Wickstrom, and Barb Wickstrom. The remarkable Plainsman Gord Howe was a generous source of help and advice in so many ways that he escapes categorization.

I am very grateful to the librarians of the Hudson's Bay Company Archives for their expert help. At the University of Regina Library, Larry McDonald led me on voyages of archives discovery in the underground vaults. Ken Dalgarno searched out materials on my behalf at the Moose Jaw City Library. Cartographer Phillip Judge both drew and advised on the maps for this book with patient professionalism. Randall Jones and George F. Thompson guided the book through to publication with quiet skill. The good judgment of my editors, Marie Blanchard, Lee Sioles, and Juliana McCarthy, improved the text. John Tarrant, Barbara Maher, Robin Haynes, Graham Bentham, and Fred Vine all advised and supported my years of research. I also thank the many unnamed individuals who in some manner aided me. Often I marvelled at the kindness of strangers.

The Nuffield Foundation, the University of East Anglia, the Royal Saskatchewan Museum, and the Canadian Plains Research Center supported various aspects of my research. One final great institution, my family, supported my endeavours throughout.

Biographic Notes

ABBEY, EDWARD (1927–1989): Abbey wrote several books extolling the wilderness of the American West. His outspoken purist views made him a hero to conservationists, but Montana ranchers threatened to lynch him for campaigning against cattle grazing on federal lands.

ATTILA (THE HUN) (circa 406–453): Attila organized a series of devastating raids on the western and eastern remnants of the Roman Empire and exacted thousands of kilograms of gold in tribute. Marriage he found more challenging than the Empire; the night after his wedding ceremony Attila died in his sleep.

BATTY, JOSEPH (?–1906): Batty was an expert huntsman. Specializing in taxidermy, he was what contemporaries called a "natural history collector."

BUDD, HENRY (circa 1812–1875): The handsome Reverend Budd, named *Sakcewescam* in Cree, was the first Native in North America to be ordained an Anglican priest. Much loved by his congregation, he wrote in fine English and preached in eloquent Cree.

BUFFALO-BIRD-WOMAN (circa 1839–circa 1925): Buffalo-bird-woman, named *Maxidiwiac Waheenee* in Hidatsa, was Gilbert Wilson's main informant on the life of the Hidatsa Indians. At the age of about seventy her memory of childhood days was splendid and she could dictate details for nine hours at a stretch.

CHAMPLAIN, SAMUEL DE (1567–1635): Champlain explored the St. Lawrence River and was quick to adopt the Indian canoe for inland travel. Under difficult circumstances his persistence ensured the founding of New France.

COCKING, MATTHEW (1743–1799): In 1772 and again in 1774 Cocking went inland from Hudson Bay to encourage Indian trade with the Hudson's Bay Company and to spy out the French-Canadian competition. He left an excellent record of prairie landscape, wildlife, and vegetation.

CORONADO, FRANCISCO (1510–1554): In 1540 Coronado set off north from Mexico with an expeditionary force of three hundred Spanish, plus the hundreds of Indians, slaves, horses, sheep, pigs, and cattle that his men needed to survive in unknown territory. He discovered the Grand Canyon and travelled north as far as present-day Kansas. The first European to see the Plains, he was also the first to be disappointed, for he failed to find gold.

CORTÉS, HERNÁN (1485–1547): With a small detachment of soldiers, sixteen horses, and a cunning understanding of human nature, Cortés wangled his way to the top of the Aztec Empire in 1519. In later years politics and the scheming of rival conquistadors ground him back down.

COWIE, ISAAC (1848–1917): In 1867, on his arrival in Hudson Bay from Scotland, Cowie's future "bloody enemies" (mosquitoes) came out to greet him while his ship was still beyond sight of land. Cowie was soon sent inland by the Hudson's Bay Company to work as a trader in the Qu'Appelle Valley. The good-humoured disposition that emerges from his vignettes of the closing days of the prairie fur trade served him well in his post.

DARWIN, CHARLES (1809–1882): Darwin's famous *On the Origin of Species*, which presented his conclusions on evolution and natural selection, was based on his many observations during the voyage of the *Beagle*. Sadly for one who so clearly loved the many landscapes he encountered on his long voyage, Darwin never left Britain a second time.

DEKKERS, MIDAS (1946–): A popular writer and broadcaster in Holland, Dekkers denounces the Western obsession with youth and perfect bodies. Instead, he encourages people to see the bright side of death and degeneration.

DICKINSON, JAMES (? – ?): Dickinson was surveyor and engineer to Henry Hind's expedition. In 1858 he split from Hind's party and explored the Qu'Appelle River from Fort Qu'Appelle downstream to its junction with the Assiniboine, the same route I followed.

DODGE, RICHARD (1827–1895): Dodge spent many years in army service on the American Plains. He was a passionate observer of both the land and its people and an outspoken critic of the injustices perpetrated against the Indian nations. They were, he said, "next to the crime of slavery the foulest blot" on the American government.

DODGE, THEODORE (1842–1909): Dodge was a military historian with an interest in horsemanship.

FIDLER, PETER (1769–1822): Fit and robust, Fidler was an accomplished explorer and cartographer on behalf of the Hudson's Bay Company. He kept meticulous journals and was a keen student of the land and its people. Often he engaged the North West Company in sharp competition at the frontiers of the fur trade, usually coming off the worse for it.

FLEMING, JOHN (1835–1876): Fleming was draftsman and assistant surveyor to Henry Hind's expedition. In 1858 he split from Hind's main party to survey the Saskatchewan River from Fort à la Corne downstream to Lake Winnipeg. His party endured much bad weather and near-starvation, but Fleming's cheerful, steady nature saw the journey through.

FROBISHER, MARTIN (1535–1594): Frobisher explored the Arctic in 1576, 1577, and 1578 in search of gold or a northwest passage. He advanced as far as Hudson Bay but failed in both his objectives.

GAYTON, DON (1946–): Gayton, a rangeland scientist, has written numerous fine essays on grassland science, management, and philosophy.

GENGHIS KHAN (circa 1162–1227): Genghis consolidated the factious nomadic tribes of the Mongolian Steppes and built an empire extending from China into central Europe. He believed that the Mongol warrior nobility should remain on the Steppes while exacting tribute from neighbouring conquered peoples. The system broke down as Mongol administrators were corrupted (or civilized) by the settled life of their various subject peoples.

GOGOL, NIKOLAI (1809–1852): A humorist and novelist, Gogol had great affection for the common folk and for the traditions and landscapes of his boyhood home, the Ukrainian countryside.

GUARESCHI, GIOVANNI (1908–1968): Guareschi wrote a series of lighthearted books centered on human fallibility. His love of his home landscape, the villages of the Po Valley, shines through his writing.

HARMON, DANIEL (1778–1843): A trader with the North West Company, Harmon left a diary of sixteen years of service, principally in the prairie. His moral and religious convictions were frequently challenged by the rough-and-ready nature of life on the prairie. He loved the outdoors and got on well with the Native peoples and most of his fellow traders, but was often plagued by the loneliness of the trader's life.

HENDRY, ANTHONY (1725–?): In 1754, in the employ of the Hudson's Bay Company, Hendry ventured inland and farther west from the Bay than any previous European, travelling on foot across the prairie. Much of his subsequent report was disbelieved, especially his insistence that the Plains Indians rode horses. In bitterness he quit the company in 1762.

HENRY, ALEXANDER ("the Elder"—where "Henry" or "Alexander Henry" alone appears in the text "Alexander Henry the Younger," described below, is intended) (1739–1824): Henry the Elder was a shareholder in the North West Company. An astute observer of Indian life, he got on well with most people and traded widely in both eastern and western Canada, ending life as a Montreal auctioneer.

HENRY, ALEXANDER ("the Younger") (circa 1765–1814): Henry the Younger left a vast personal journal covering fifteen years of service in the North West Company. He disliked most people: the Indians he traded with, his competitors, and his employees. Although unsympathetic to the people and the land, he understood the business of trading like few others and his accounts are free of embellishment or romance.

HERODOTUS (circa 484 B.C.–circa 425 B.C.): In recognition of his achievements in writing the first great narrative history, Herodotus is called by some the Father of History and by others the Father of Lies. The conduct of the Greco-Persian wars was for him factual proof that "pride comes before a fall."

HIND, HENRY (1823–1908): A University of Toronto professor, Hind was commissioned by the Canadian government in 1857 to explore the Canadian prairies and to report on their suitability for settlement. Hind was prejudiced about the Indians and Métis but his report contains a mass of more objective detail about the land itself. Occasionally, despite his analytical training, Hind was overwhelmed by the scale and beauty of the prairies.

HUDSON, WILLIAM (1841–1922): Hudson grew up roaming the Pampas around his parents' sheep farm. A writer and keen-eyed naturalist, he accepted the natural world without prejudice.

KANE, PAUL (1810–1871): A professional painter, Kane ventured west onto the Canadian prairies in 1846 and created the most important pictorial record of Native and European life of the time. His field sketches were lively in line, while his paintings were vibrant with colour.

KELSEY, HENRY (circa 1667–1724): Kelsey was a Hudson's Bay Company employee and the first European on the northern prairie. In 1690 he ventured inland from the Bay and penetrated beyond the Saskatchewan River. He enjoyed writing his reports, which included sightings of buffalo and Plains grizzlies, in bad rhyme.

KURZ, RUDOLPH (1818–1871): Kurz was trained as a painter in Europe, but made his day-to-day living as a clerk in fur trading posts on the Missouri River. Sympathetic to the Indian way of life, he travelled in hope, asking: "Man's habitations spread over the whole earth; there are churches and schoolhouses without number; yet where are men found dwelling together in unity?"

LEE, ROBERT (1956–): Lee is a newspaper columnist who writes on politics and western Canadian issues.

LE JEUNE, FATHER PAUL (1591–1664): Le Jeune was the founder of the Jesuit missions in New France and was responsible for the first eleven volumes of the *Relations*, the Jesuit reports of the New World. Extremely devout, he loved the land and its people.

LEWIS, MERIWETHER (1774–1809) and WILLIAM CLARK (1770–1838): Lewis and Clark held joint command of the 1804–1806 government-financed exploratory expedition from St. Louis to the Pacific and back. They dispelled ideas of an easy passage to the Pacific and amassed a wealth of detailed observations of the West.

LORENZ, KONRAD (1903–1989): An Austrian, Lorenz was the founder of the scientific study of animal behaviour. Most famously, Lorenz discovered "imprinting" by observing how goslings and ducklings mistook him for their mother if he appeared at the right stage in their early development. He won the Nobel Prize in 1973.

MACDONALD, JOHN (circa 1774–1866): A full North West Company partner in about 1799, MacDonald took over Fort Espérance on the Qu'Appelle River from John Macdonell. The boastful and brave MacDonald then abandoned the post after trouble with Indians and built another post farther upstream—only to be ambushed on the downstream run with the winter's furs. On account of his crippled arm he was nicknamed *"Bras Croche."*

MACDONELL, JOHN (1768–1850): A North West Company trader, Macdonell arrived at Fort Espérance on the Qu'Appelle River in 1793 to become the third proprietor. He became a *bourgeois*, a full company partner, in about 1796. To his men he was known as *"Le Prêtre"* ("The Priest") on account of the piety he inflicted on them.

MARQUETTE, FATHER JACQUES (1637–1675): The Jesuit Marquette and the adventurer Louis Jolliet were directed by the governor of New France to explore the Mississippi River. Marquette died during his return along the shore of Lake Michigan at the mouth of the river since called Père Marquette.

MASON, BILL (1929–1988): Mason is Canada's most famous modern wilderness canoeist. His handbooks and films remain invaluable guides to the art of canoe travel.

MAXIMILIAN VON WIED (Prince) (1782–1867): A naturalist and ethnologist respected for his earlier Brazilian explorations, Maximilian travelled the Missouri River as a guest of the American Fur Company. His careful journal notes of the country west of the Mississippi are second in importance only to those of Lewis and Clark.

McDONALD, ARCHIBALD (1836–1915): A man of authority, McDonald was active in the transition from a fur trading to an agricultural economy. He was in charge of the Hudson's Bay Company's Fort Qu'Appelle post during Isaac Cowie's apprenticeship.

McKAY, JOHN (1792–1877): The Indians admired McKay for his skills as a horseman, swordsman, and marksman, and liked him for his just and generous trading. His employer, the Hudson's Bay Company, considered him extravagant.

MONDRIAN, PIET (1872–1944): In search of balance and purity of form Mondrian became a leading exponent of abstract art. His work became based on straight lines, right angles, and blocks of solid colour.

MUGGERIDGE, KEN (1955–): Muggeridge is a prairie gentleman with an outstanding knowledge of things mechanical.

OVALLE, FATHER ALONSO DE (1601–1651): The Jesuit de Ovalle was famous as an orator and intellectual. Born in the New World, he loved its landscapes and its native inhabitants. His elegant writing style earned him the title "Father of Chilean prose."

REMINGTON, FREDERIC (1861–1909): Remington was an illustrator, painter, and occasional correspondent on life in the American West. He had a fine eye for detail.

RUNDLE, ROBERT ("Rundell") (1811–1896): The Welsh Reverend Rundle loved to travel the prairies from his base at Fort Edmonton. A Wesleyan missionary, he got on well with the Catholic "competition."

SCHMIDT, ULRICH (circa 1510–circa 1579): Under contract to Flemish merchants, Schmidt shipped with the Spanish to South America in the hopes of trading for gold or silver. After twenty years abroad he returned to Antwerp in 1554 and wrote of his New World adventures.

SETON, ERNEST (1860–1946): Seton trailed and hunted in prairie Manitoba for many years. He was an early, and influential, conservationist.

SHEVCHENKO, TARAS (1814–1861): A committed nationalist sentenced to exile for his views by Tsar Nicholas, Shevchenko was the foremost poet of nineteenth-century Ukraine. Shevchenko was born a serf, but a friend's painting bought him his freedom.

SIMPSON, SIR GEORGE (1792–1860): Active in the turbulent years before and after the merger of the Hudson's Bay Company with its bitter rival, the North West Company, Simpson became the most famous governor in the long history of "The Honourable Company." He advanced the firm's interests unflaggingly and was a tireless traveller.

SMITH, G. HUBERT (1908–1972): Smith was an anthropologist concerned with establishing the route La Vérendrye took across the northern prairies. Against his will, Smith's conclusions led to the disestablishment of Vérendrye National Monument in North Dakota.

STEGNER, WALLACE (1909–1993): Stegner wrote both fiction and nonfiction about the prairies, winning the Pulitzer Prize in 1972. He was deeply concerned with the effect of the open landscape on settlers and remained ambivalent about the prairies to his death. Of his boyhood hometown on the edge of the Saskatchewan Cypress Hills, he wrote, "Give it a thousand years."

STEINBECK, JOHN (1902–1968): A Nobel Prize winner, Steinbeck wrote of the fate of failed Plains farmers in the dust bowl years with both sympathy and relentless realism.

SUTHERLAND, JAMES (1778–1844): Sutherland was a Hudson's Bay Company trader. Having survived the troubled years of fur trade competition, Sutherland prospered in the calm after the merger of 1821 with the North West Company, rising to become a justice of the peace.

SUTHERLAND, JOHN (? – ?): Sutherland served in the Hudson's Bay Company from 1778 to 1812. In 1794, tiring of his unrewarded "life of fear" in service, he wrote: "If the Governer will not smile on me at my return now I will resign the Hon:[ble] Companys Service, for I am sure there is hardly any employment which if pursued with atention will not yeald an income sufficent for the necessary uses of life, and no Revenue is so great as to be proof against Extravagance."

TAMERLANE (1336–1405): Tamerlane, or Timur the Lame, was the last great imperial conqueror of grasslands Asia. While famed for his barbarity (his men built pyramids of skulls after a successful sacking), he also beautified his capital, Samarkand, and supported the arts. He remained determinedly nomadic all his life.

TRUDEAU, JOSEPH PHILIPPE PIERRE YVES ELLIOTT (1919–2000): A prime minister famed for his arrogance and intellect, Trudeau was convinced that Canada's vast wilderness landscape constituted an essential element of Canadian identity. Canoeing, he maintained, was the best way to experience that landscape, and he never tired of urging his compatriots to take up the paddle.

VÉRENDRYE, PIERRE GAULTIER DE VARENNES, SIEUR DE LA (1685–1749): La Vérendrye and his sons built a string of French trading posts from Rainy Lake west to the Assiniboine River. He penetrated farther west than any previous trader and almost single-handedly broke the monopoly of the Hudson's Bay Company in the Northwest—all at his own expense. For his troubles he was severely criticized by the authorities in New France for failing to find "the western sea."

WILSON, GILBERT (1868–1930): Wilson visited the Hidatsa Indians for a few months every year between 1908 and 1918. Not content with simply cataloging and cross-classifying beliefs and artifacts, he was one of the first anthropologists to try to understand the nature of life from the philosophic standpoint of his informants.

XERXES (circa 519 B.C.–465 B.C.): Called "the Great," Xerxes ruled Persia, Babylon, and Egypt, yet is most remembered for the spectacular failure of his invasion of Greece.

Chapter Notes

Chapter One

I use oceanic metaphors to describe the Plains in this chapter and throughout the book. This follows an old tradition, for comparisons with the sea are rife in prairie writings from the earliest reports to today. Written in unhurried Edwardian prose, the most overt and beautiful comparison of the twin sisters, the grasslands and the sea, is William Quayle's *The Prairie and the Sea*.

Steven Bourassa's *The Aesthetics of Landscape* describes which landscapes we are genetically programmed to prefer and which to reject. The book also outlines prospect-refuge theory, which explains the reasons behind our landscape preferences and the differences between male and female views. Trevor Herriot's *River in a Dry Land* is a recent collection of memoirs and stories of the human and natural history of the Qu'Appelle watershed. An excellent layperson's guide to the geology and geography of the Qu'Appelle Valley, sadly now difficult to find, is E. Christiansen's *Fort Qu'Appelle Geolog*.

Chapters Two and Three

There are many readable accounts of animal domestication. One of the best is Juliet Clutton-Brock's *A Natural History of Domesticated Animals*. The classic, technical account of different dog races and their uses in the pre-European Americas is Glover Allen's "Dogs of the American Aborigines." David Olesen's *Cold Nights, Fast Trails* describes the genesis of the husky and its modern use as a sled dog. Buffalo-bird-woman's detailed verbatim accounts of the construction and use of both dog and horse travois are in Gilbert Wilson's "The Horse and the Dog in Hidatsa Culture." An excellent, readable account of dog psychology and sociology is Konrad Lorenz's *Man Meets Dog*.

A technical account of my journeys with Serge is "Replicating Dog Travois Travel on the Northern Plains." An excellent holistic account of how and where people lived on the Plains in the Dog Age is Douglas Bamforth's *Ecology and Human Organization on the Great Plains*. A. W. Rasporich describes the Hamona experiment in "Utopian Ideals and Community Settlements in Western Canada."

A book remains to be written documenting the European encounter with the mosquitoes, black flies, no-see-ems, tabanids, and other biting, flying insects of North America. A good starting point would be the Jesuit missionary Paul du Poisson's 1727 report of his travails on the heartland river of the continent: "But the greatest torture—without which everything else would have been only a recreation, but which passes all belief, and could never be imagined in France unless it had been experienced—is the mosquitoes, the cruel persecution of the mosquitoes . . . This little creature has caused more swearing since the French came to *Mississipi*, than had been done before that time in all the rest of the world."

Chapters Four and Five

Andreas Schroeder's *Dust Ship Glory* is a short novel loosely based on Sukanen's labors. Ronald Rees's *New and Naked Land* is a fine account of the shock experienced by immigrants to the prairies arriving in a land "from which the hand of God had been withdrawn." Rees also describes the propaganda campaigns undertaken in Europe by the Canadian government to attract immigrants and considers the misplaced cult of the tree on the prairies.

The best overall account of the canoe and its many forms and uses in North America is *The Canoe* by Philip Shackelton and Kenneth Roberts. There are many accounts of the fur trade in Canada, but the best succinct depiction of fur trade logistics and canoe transport is Eric Morse's *Fur Trade Routes of Canada*. The most comprehensive study, overwhelming in its detail, is *The Fur Trade in Canada* by Harold Innis. Alexander Henry's *Manuscript Journals* and Daniel Harmon's *Sixteen Years in the Indian Country* give detailed accounts of day-to-day life for fur traders around 1800 to 1810. In an anecdotal style Isaac Cowie describes the final days of the Plains fur trade in *The Company of Adventurers*.

A technical account of my canoe journey is "The Canoe as Failure on the Canadian Plains." Edward Abbey's damning description of cattle in the American West is in *Beyond the Wall*.

Chapters Six and Seven

A clear, popular account of the theory that human hunting wiped out New World megafauna is in Jared Diamond's *The Rise and Fall of the Third Chimpanzee*. Recent modelling work by John Alroy, "A Multispecies Overkill Simulation of the End-Pleistocene Megafaunal Mass Extinction," supports the theory. Frank Roe's *The Indian and the Horse* describes the spread of the horse across the Plains and details the many uses to which it was put by Native North Americans. Roe supports the idea that the horse allowed selective, and therefore sustainable, buffalo hunting. John Ewers in *The Horse in Blackfoot Indian Culture* and Buffalo-bird-woman in Gilbert Wilson's "The Horse and the Dog in Hidatsa Culture" provide the best descriptions of how to build a horse travois. No, I do not approve of Genghis Khan's ethnic cleansing plan, though I stand in awe of his grassland vision.

A technical account of my horse travels is "Replicating Horse and Travois Travel." Walter Webb's classic work, *The Great Plains,* includes a history of barbed wire and the explosive expansion of fencing that destroyed the horseman's Plains mobility. Richard Dodge's fascinating stories of Plains navigation are in *The Plains of the Great West and Their Inhabitants.*

Chapter Eight

In "Beauty and Nothingness" Neil Evernden summarizes the difficulty of communicating the experience of prairie, as it is, he says, "an experience, not an object—a sensation, not a view."

References

Abbey, Edward. *Beyond the Wall: Essays from the Outside*. New York: Holt, Rinehart, and Winston, 1984.

Allen, Glover. "Dogs of the American Aborigines." *Bulletin of the Museum of Comparative Zoology* 63, no. 9 (1920), 431–541.

Alroy, John. "A Multispecies Overkill Simulation of the End-Pleistocene Megafaunal Mass Extinction." *Science* 292, no. 5523 (2001), 1893–96.

Ashley, Clifford. *The Ashley Book of Knots*. London: Faber and Faber, 1947.

Bamforth, Douglas. *Ecology and Human Organization on the Great Plains*. New York: Plenum Press, 1988.

Barris, Theodore. *Fire Canoe*. Toronto: McClelland and Stewart, 1977.

Batty, Joseph. *How to Hunt and Trap*. 2d ed. New York: Orange Judd, 1882.

Bourassa, Steven. *The Aesthetics of Landscape*. New York: Belhaven Press, 1991.

Breen, David. *The Canadian Prairie West and the Ranching Frontier, 1874–1924*. Toronto: University of Toronto Press, 1983.

Canals Frau, Salvador. *Las Poblaciones Indígenas de la Argentina*. Buenos Aires: Editorial Sudamericana, 1953.

Champlain, Samuel de. *Voyages to New France*. Ottawa: Oberon Press, 1971.

Christiansen, E., et al. *Fort Qu'Appelle Geolog*. Saskatoon: Saskatchewan Culture and Youth and Parks Canada, 1981.

Clutton-Brock, Juliet. *A Natural History of Domesticated Animals*. Cambridge: Cambridge University Press, 1987.

Cocking, Matthew. "Journal of Matthew Cocking from York Factory to the Blackfeet Country 1772–73." *Proceedings and Transactions of the Royal Society of Canada*, 3d ser., vol. 2, sec. 2 (1908), 89–121.

Coronado, Francisco. See Winship, George.

Cowie, Isaac. *The Company of Adventurers*. Toronto: William Briggs, 1913.

Darwin, Charles. *Journal of Researches into the Geology and Natural History of the Various Countries Visited during the Voyage of H.M.S. Beagle round the World.* 1845. Reprint, London: J. M. Dent, 1906. (For chapter 1.)

———. *On the Origin of Species.* London: John Murray, 1859. (For biographic note.)

Dekkers, Midas. *The Way of All Flesh.* New York: Farrar, Straus, and Giroux, 2000.

Diamond, Jared. *The Rise and Fall of the Third Chimpanzee.* London: Radius, 1991.

Dickinson, James. See Hind, Henry.

Dodge, Richard. *Our Wild Indians: Thirty-three Years' Personal Experience among the Red Men of the Great West.* Hartford, Conn.: A. D. Worthington, 1882. (For chapter 6 quotation and for biographic note.)

———. *The Plains of the Great West and Their Inhabitants.* New York: Putnam's, 1877. (For chapter 7.)

Dodge, Theodore. "Some American Riders." *Harper's New Monthly Magazine* 82 (1891), 849–62.

Doyle, Rodger. "Christian Differences." *Scientific American* 281, no. 1 (1999), 26.

Evernden, Neil. "Beauty and Nothingness: Prairie as Failed Resource." *Landscape* 27, no. 3 (1983), 1–8.

Ewers, John. *The Horse in Blackfoot Indian Culture* (Bureau of American Ethnology Bulletin 159). Washington, D.C.: Smithsonian Institution, 1955.

Fidler, Peter. "Brandon House Journal, 1815–1816." B22/a/19, Hudson's Bay Company Archives, Winnipeg.

Fitzgerald, Charles. *China: A Short Cultural History.* London: Century Hutchinson, 1986.

Fleming, John. See Hind, Henry.

Frobisher, Martin. See Allen, Glover.

Gayton, Don. *The Wheatgrass Mechanism.* Saskatoon: Fifth House, 1990.

Gogol, Nikolai. *Taras Bulba and Other Tales.* London: Everyman's Library, 1918.

Guareschi, Giovanni. *The Little World of Don Camillo.* New York: Farrar, Straus, and Giroux, 1950.

Haines, Francis. "The Northward Spread of Horses among the Plains Indians." *American Anthropologist* 40 (1938), 129–97.

Harmon, Daniel. *Sixteen Years in the Indian Country.* 1820. Reprint, Toronto: Macmillan, 1957.

Henderson, Norman. "The Canoe as Failure on the Canadian Plains." *Great Plains Research* 6 (1996), 3–23.

———. "Replicating Dog Travois Travel on the Northern Plains." *Plains Anthropologist* 39 (1994), 145–59.

———. "Replicating Horse and Travois Travel." *Prairie Forum* 21 (1996), 137–47.

Hendry, Anthony. "The Journal of Anthony Hendry, 1754–55." *Proceedings and Transactions of the Royal Society of Canada* 3d ser., vol. 1, sec. 2 (1907), 307–64.

Henry, Alexander (the Elder). *Travels and Adventures in Canada and the Indian Territories between the Year 1760 and 1776.* 1809. Reprint, Rutland, Vt.: C. E. Tuttle, 1969.

Henry, Alexander (the Younger), and David Thompson. *The Manuscript Journals of Alexander Henry and of David Thompson, 1799–1814.* 2 vols. Edited by Elliott Coues. Minneapolis: Ross and Haines, 1897.

Herodotus. *The History.* Translated by David Grene. Chicago: University of Chicago Press, 1987. (For chapter 6 quotation. For chapter 7 quotation, see Luce, T. J.)

Herriot, Trevor. *River in a Dry Land: A Prairie Passage.* Toronto: Stoddart, 2000.

Hind, Henry Youle. *Narrative of the Canadian Red River Exploring Expedition of 1857 and of the Assinniboine and Saskatchewan Exploring Expedition of 1858.* London: Longman, Green, Longman, and Roberts, 1860.

Hudson, William. *Far Away and Long Ago.* London: Dent and Sons, 1918.

Innis, Harold. *The Fur Trade in Canada.* 1930. Rev. ed., Toronto: University of Toronto Press, 1956.

Kane, Paul. *Wanderings of an Artist among the Indians of North America.* 1859. Reprint, Edmonton: Hurtig, 1968.

Kenton, Edna, ed. *The Jesuit Relations and Allied Documents.* 1925. Reprint, New York: Vanguard Press, 1954.

Kurz, Rudolph. *Journal of Rudolph Friederich Kurz* (Bureau of American Ethnology Bulletin 115). Washington, D.C.: Smithsonian Institution, 1937.

Lee, Robert. "Why does Ottawa consider a canoe more Canadian than a cowboy? Eh?" *Globe and Mail,* August 6, 1994.

Le Jeune, Paul. "Relation 1637." In *Jesuit Relations and Allied Documents: Travels and Explorations of the Jesuit Missionaries in New France, 1610–1791,* vol. 12. Edited by Reuben Thwaites. Cleveland: Burrows Bros., 1896–1901.

Lewis, Meriwether, and William Clark. *History of the Expedition under the Command of Lewis and Clark.* 4 vols. Edited by Elliott Coues. New York: Harper, 1893.

Lorenz, Konrad. *Man Meets Dog.* 1950. Reprint, London: Methuen, 1954.

Luce, T. J. *The Greek Historians.* London: Routledge, 1997.

MacDonald, John. See Morton, A. S.

Macdonell, John. "The Diary of John Macdonell." In *Five Fur Traders of the Northwest.* Edited by C. M. Gates. Minneapolis: University of Minnesota Press, 1933. (For chapter 4 quotation.)

————. "Journal" (1793–1795). In *Les bourgeois de la Compagnie du Nord-Ouest: récits de voyages, lettres, et rapports inédits relatifs au nord-ouest canadien,* 1st ser. Edited by L. R.

Masson. 1889. Reprint, New York: Antiquarian Press, 1960. (For chapter 7 quotation.)

MacKay, Douglas. *The Honourable Company.* London: Cassell, 1937.

Mandelbaum, David. "The Plains Cree." *Anthropological Papers of the American Museum of Natural History* 37, pt. 2 (1940), 155–316.

Marquette, Jacques. "First Voyage." In *Jesuit Relations and Allied Documents: Travels and Explorations of the Jesuit Missionaries in New France, 1610–1791,* vol. 59. Edited by Reuben Thwaites. Cleveland: Burrows Bros., 1896–1901.

Martin, Paul. "The Discovery of America." *Science* 179, no. 4077 (1973), 969–74.

Maximilian von Wied (Prince). "Travels in the Interior of North America, 1830." In *Early Western Travels,* vols. 22–24. Edited by Reuben Thwaites. Cleveland: A. H. Clark, 1906.

McCauley, Martin. *Khrushchev and the Development of Soviet Agriculture: The Virgin Land Programme, 1953–1964.* London: Macmillan, 1976.

McKay, John. "Fort Ellice Post Journal, 1812–1813." B63/a/2, Hudson's Bay Company Archives, Winnipeg.

McNaughton, S. J. "Grazing Lawns: Animals in Herds, Plant Form, and Coevolution." *American Naturalist* 124 (1984), 863–86.

Morgan, R. Grace. "Beaver Mythology, Beaver Ecology." (Ph.D. dissertation, University of Alberta, Edmonton, 1991).

Morse, Eric. *Fur Trade Routes of Canada / Then and Now.* Ottawa: Queen's Printer, 1968.

Morton, A. S. "Five Fur Trade Posts on the Lower Qu'Appelle River, 1787–1819." *Transactions of the Royal Society of Canada,* 3d ser., vol. 35, sec. 2 (1941), 81–93.

Mullin, L. J., Eldon Owens, and Dick Meacher. *Tom Sukanen and His Ship.* Moose Jaw, Sask.: Ferguson Printing, 1976.

Nelson, J. G. *The Last Refuge.* Montreal: Harvest House, 1973.

Olesen, David. *Cold Nights, Fast Trails.* Minocqua, Wis.: Northword Press, 1989.

Ovalle, Alonso de. *Histórica Relación del Reino de Chile.* 1646. Reprint, Santiago de Chile: Editorial Universitaria, Universidad de Chile, 1969.

Poisson, Paul du. "Letter from Father du Poisson, missionary to the Akensas ... " In *Jesuit Relations and Allied Documents: Travels and Explorations of the Jesuit Missionaries in New France, 1610–1791,* vol. 67. Edited by Reuben Thwaites. Cleveland: Burrows Bros., 1896–1901.

Quayle, William. *The Prairie and the Sea.* Cincinnati: Jennings and Graham, 1905.

Rasporich, A. W. "Utopian Ideals and Community Settlements in Western Canada 1880–1914." In *The Prairie West.* Edited by R. Francis and H. Palmer. Edmonton: University of Alberta Press, 1985.

Rees, Ronald. *New and Naked Land: Making the Prairies Home.* Saskatoon: Western Producer, 1988.

Remington, Frederic. "Horses of the Plains." *Century Magazine* 37 (1889), 332–43.

Rock, David. *Argentina, 1516–1982.* Berkeley: University of California Press, 1985.

Roe, Frank. *The Indian and the Horse.* Norman: University of Oklahoma Press, 1955.

———. *The North American Buffalo.* Toronto: University of Toronto Press, 1970.

Saskatchewan Environment and Resource Management. *Saskatchewan's State of the Environment Report 1997: Our Prairie Ecozone Our Agricultural Heartland.* Regina: SERM, 1997.

Schmidt, Ulrich. "Voyage of Ulrich Schmidt to the Rivers La Plata and Paraguai." In *The Conquest of the River Plate, 1535–1555.* Edited by Luís Domínguez. London: Hakluyt Society, 1891.

Schroeder, Andreas. *Dust Ship Glory.* Toronto: Doubleday, 1986.

Scobie, James. *Argentina: A City and a Nation.* 2d ed. New York: Oxford University Press, 1971.

Seton, Ernest Thompson. *The Arctic Prairies.* 1911. Reprint, New York: Scribner, 1920. (For chapter 3 quotation.)

———. *Wild Animals I Have Known.* 1898. Reprint, New York: Hodder and Stoughton, 1914.

Shackelton, Philip, and Kenneth Roberts. *The Canoe.* Toronto: Macmillan, 1983.

Shevchenko, Taras. *Taras Shevchenko: Selected Works, Poetry and Prose.* Moscow: Progress Publishers, 1979.

Simpson, George. "Official Reports to the Governor and Committee in London 31 July 1822." D.4/85, Hudson's Bay Company Archives, Winnipeg. (For chapter 4 quotation.)

———. "Journals 1824–25." D.3/1, Hudson's Bay Company Archives, Winnipeg. (For chapter 7 quotation.)

Sludsky, A. A. "Saiga in Kazakhstan" (in Russian). *Proceedings of the Institute of Zoology, Academy of Sciences of Kazakh SSR* 4 (1955), 18–55.

Smith, G. Hubert. *The Explorations of the La Vérendryes in the Northern Plains, 1738–43.* Edited by W. R. Wood. Lincoln: University of Nebraska Press, 1980.

Stegner, Wallace. *Wolf Willow.* Lincoln: University of Nebraska Press, 1952.

Sutherland, John. "Journal and Remarks at River Kapell, 1793–94." B63/a/1, Hudson's Bay Company Archives, Winnipeg. (For "thumb" quotation.)

———. "Remarks and Observations on Traveling Inland." B63/a/1, Hudson's Bay Company Archives, Winnipeg. (For "sticks and stumps" quotation and for biographic note.)

Thomas, Elizabeth. *The Hidden Life of Dogs.* Boston: Houghton Mifflin, 1993.

Thwaites, Reuben, ed. *Jesuit Relations and Allied Documents: Travels and Explorations of the Jesuit Missionaries in New France, 1610–1791.* 73 vols. Cleveland: Burrows Bros., 1896–1901.

Trudeau, Pierre Elliott. "Exhaustion and Fulfilment: The Ascetic in a Canoe." 1944. In *Wilderness Canada.* Edited by Bordon Spears. Toronto: Clark Irwin, 1970.

Vérendrye, Pierre Gaultier de Varennes, sieur de la. See Smith, G. Hubert.

Wallace, William, ed. *The Dictionary of Canadian Biography.* Toronto: Macmillan, 1926.

Webb, Walter. *The Great Plains.* Boston: Ginn, 1931.

Webster, Michael. "Rambo Grass." *Equinox* 12, no. 4 (1993), 95.

Wilson, Gilbert. "The Horse and the Dog in Hidatsa Culture." *Anthropological Papers of the American Museum of Natural History* 15, pt. 2 (1924), 125–331.

Winship, George. *The Coronado Expedition, 1540–1542* (Bureau of American Ethnology 14th Annual Report). Washington, D.C.: Smithsonian Institution, 1896.

Index

pipe, 104–5

pipeline, 27

pitch, 71–72, 77

Plains: all-levelling, 126; alternative history, 136; ancient, 49; burned, 157–58; Canadian, 2, 157; catastrophes, 160–61, 176–78; Celtic, 155; ecology, 111; essence of, vii; euphoria, 122; as Hell, 65; landscape, vii–viii; madness, 164; moisture balance, 77; northern, 18, 57, 131–32, 152; Patagonian, 9; question of belonging to, 122; rarely flat, vii; river names, 83; rivers, 67, 83, 103; scale of, 122–23, 170; silence, 170; sister grasslands of, ix, 160; sun, 159, 170; truly great, 145; vision of paradise, 130; . *See also* grassland; prairie

Plains Indians: and beaver, 115; broken, 136; and bull boats, 67; and dogs, 14–18; and horses, 130–32, 134–36; hunters, 115, 132, 135; and mosquitoes, 30; relations with fur traders, 72–74; seasonal migrations, 48, 130; self-sufficiency, 72–73, 130, 176; setting fires, 158; vision of paradise, 130; and water, 152–53. *See also* Dog Age peoples; Indians; Native peoples

Pleistocene, 128

plough: disaster of, 176; "rain follows," 177

plover, 27, 121

Po River, 84

poisoning, insecticide, 155

pony, 131–32, 139–40

poplar, 11, 22, 36, 41, 62, 105

portage: Crooked Lake weir, 106; electric fence, 91; Great Falls, 159; Katepwa Lake weir, 83; between meanders, 100; Round Lake weir, 108

Portage la Prairie, 73

potash, 177

prairie: accidents, 151; aerial view of, 178–80; air, 5, 7; alien, 122; autumn colors, 61; brief summer, 89; burned, 157–58; Canadian, 67, 130, 161; catastrophes, 159–161; climate, 27, 75, 177; culture, 111; described in the nega-

tive, 9; dress codes, 82; egalitarianism, 57; environment, 159; essence of, 175; euphoria, 123; ever-present wind of, 126; freedom, 169; gold, 155; homogeneity, 81; and horses, 127–28; incomprehensible, 122; landscape, 7–9, 12, 34, 57, 122–23, 148, 165, 175; madness 7, 65–66; Manitoba, 131, 158; native, 49, 164; navigation of, 164–65; northern, 90, 152; ocean-like, 63, 66, 105; optimism, 61, 104; perfection, 169; ploughed and fenced, 177; purest elements, 55; purity of, 175; question of belonging to, 8; reality of, 161, 176; reconciliation, 177; rivers, viii, 71, 83, 103; romance of, vii; scale of, 175; schooner, 66; silence, 122–23, 148; solitude of, 20; spirit of, 126, 161; subjugated, 111; sun, , 70, 95, 106; at sunrise and sunset, 170; tallgrass, 70; towns, 81–82, 114, 177; unfenced, 145, 168; urban, 69; vastness, 157, 169; winter, 61, 154; wool, 11, 49. *See also* grassland; Plains

Precambrian Shield, 5

Price Coulee, 146–47, 170

progress, belief in, 135

protohorses, 127

Qu'Appelle River: apportionment of, 121; bubbles, 92–93, 116; confluence with Assiniboine, 29, 60, 71, 123–24; crossing, 36–38, 102, 166–67; as drinking source, 29, 45, 112; drowned buffalo in, 158; ever-changing, 80, 116; floodplain, 10, 35, 38, 43, 88; and garbage, 95, 98, 123; headwaters, 11, 75–76; nature of, 45, 80, 83–84, 121, 123; navigability, 75; navigation history, 67, 71–72, 74–78; by night, 118; origin of, 10; rapids, 74, 76, 79, 112, 115, 121; as remnant, 11; rich with life, 89–90, 96, 109–10, 112–13, 116; seasonal flow, 75; sinuosity, 10–11, 35, 60, 72, 74–76, Qu'Appelle River (*cont.*)

78, 89–90, 93, 95, 97, 99, 105, 108–9, 112, 116–17, 121; superior to mirror, 117; watershed, 63, 124

ABOUT THE AUTHOR

NORMAN HENDERSON was born in 1960 in Saskatchewan. He studied economics and geography in Saskatchewan and in Nuremberg, Germany. Awarded a Commonwealth Scholarship, he travelled to Britain, where he completed a doctorate in environmental sciences. Henderson subsequently worked as a lecturer (assistant professor) at the University of East Anglia in Britain. Haunted by memories of his childhood landscape, he visited the sister grasslands of the Great Plains: he cycled the Hungarian *Puszta* (the westernmost edge of the Steppes) and wandered the Argentinean Pampas. He designed and taught a university course on the comparative histories, environments, and economic development of the three great temperate grasslands.

In 1998, with his wife Elaine, Henderson returned to Saskatchewan. He currently works in climate research at the University of Regina. He has published scholarly articles in many fields and regularly published editorial columns in daily newspapers in the United States, Canada, and Australia. *Rediscovering the Prairies*, his first book-length work, was originally published as *Rediscovering the Great Plains* (Johns Hopkins University Press, 2001).

The author can be contacted directly at: journeysbydog@hotmail.com.